the
Herbalist's Garden

the Herbalist's Garden

A Guided Tour of 10 Exceptional Herb Gardens
The People Who Grow Them and the Plants That Inspire Them

Shatoiya and Richard de la Tour • Photography by Saxon Holt

STOREY
BOOKS

The mission of Storey Communications
is to serve our customers by publishing practical information
that encourages personal independence in harmony with the environment.

This publication is intended to provide educational information for the reader on the covered subject. It is not intended to take the place of personalized medical counseling, diagnosis, and treatment from a trained health professional.

Edited by Deborah Balmuth and Nancy Ringer
Cover design by Meredith Maker
Photographs by Saxon Holt
Illustrations by Beverly Duncan
Text design by Carol Jessop, Black Trout Design
Book layout by Susan Bernier
Indexed by Susan Olason, Indexes & Knowledge Maps

Printed in Canada by Transcontinental Printing
10 9 8 7 6 5 4 3 2 1

Library of Congress Cataloging-in-Publication Data
De la Tour, Shatoiya.
    The herbalist's garden / Shatoiya and Richard de la Tour ; photographs by Saxon Holt.
        p.   cm.
    Includes bibliographical references (p.).
    ISBN 1-58017-294-6 (hc. : alk. paper)
    1. Herb gardens — United States.   2. Herb gardens — British Columbia — Vancouver Island. 3. Herbs — United States.   4. Herbs — British Columbia — Vancouver Island. 5. Herbalists — United States — Biography.   6. Herbalists — British Columbia — Vancouver Island — Biography. I. De la Tour, Richard. II. Title.
    SB351.H5 D42 2001
    635'.7'0973—dc21   00-056321

To all those who serve as caretakers for the land.

— Shatoiya and Richard de la Tour

I dedicate my work to where it has come from —
thank you to all the gardeners who have so generously opened
their gardens and lives to me.

— Saxon Holt

AUTHORS' ACKNOWLEDGMENTS

We thank the entire staff of Storey Books for their warmth and kind support. We especially thank Deborah Balmuth for her friendship and guidance, Nancy Ringer for being a wise and patient book midwife, Charly Smith for his knowledge, Susan Bernier for her creative work, and Nancy Kahan for being a great cheerleader. Watching Saxon Holt work was akin to being witness to a Zen master — thank you, Saxon. We also thank the gardeners in this book, as well as all the other gardeners we have been blessed to meet, for their willingness to share their experiences and their love of the land. Last, we thank those most close to us who have helped make our farm a beautiful place: Andy Ferkin, Kim Hause, Carl Kimble, Marcus, P.T., Joe, and Howie.

Contents

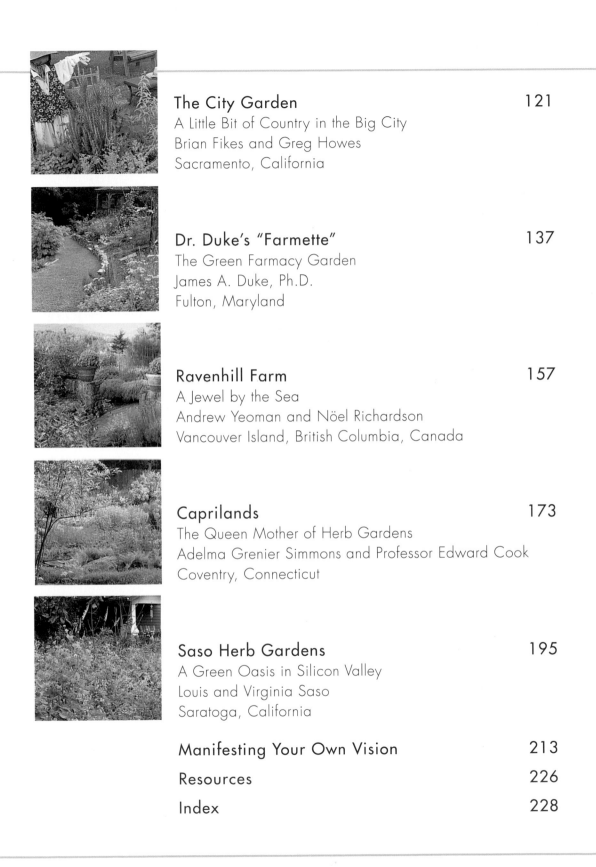

PREFACE

If we could use only two words to describe gardeners, they would be *passionate* and *spiritual*. Passion can come in many forms. Some gardeners are passionate about making perfect compost. Some grow only the most unusual varieties of plants and will search for years for specific seeds or cuttings. Some are fulfilled by creating precise moods in their landscape using particular colors and textures. Others are most interested in helping the wildness around them flourish.

Regardless of the particular bent of their passion, gardeners are all eager to show you around their personal Eden. They have been lovers sowing the seeds in the fertile earth and midwives in bringing these beings to light, and they are now proud parents watching their plants grow and sharing their experiences. Year after year, gardeners tend to their charges, and many of them actually refer to their beloved plants as children or old friends. And that's where the spirituality comes in.

When we, as humans, realize that we are not the only intelligent life on this planet, it changes us. We feel the connections and realize how our actions affect all life on the earth. To watch a fruit tree being transformed — from seeming lifelessness to a bounty of lush pink blossoms, to a vibrant ball of green leaves, then to fruit, and then to dormancy again — is to see the divine in action.

Gardeners know this. They see that all the while the tree is living its life, it is also giving and providing for other life, whether it be in the form of housing for the insects and birds, nectar for the bees, fruit for the humans and animals, or dead leaves as food for the earth. It is a vivid lesson of the great circle of life. When you are on your knees working within this circle of life, you cannot help but be touched by its silent sermon.

It has been our pleasure to travel to many gardens and visit with these stewards of the earth. We found the stories of their gardens inspiring, and we have always come home with fresh energy and attitude toward our little farm. In this book, we share with you some of our favorite green places and the people who created them. We asked these gardeners to share with us their stories and their favorite "green garden friends." In the hope that you will be encouraged to study these plants further, we have also given some of the time-honored medicinal uses for these herbs and flowers.

We hope you will see parts of yourself in each of these herb gardeners and know that you, too, can create a blessed place on earth to hold your sacred dreams.

◁ For an herb gardener, luxury is a quiet corner from which to watch the green things grow. Here, whimsical bent willow furniture stands framed by comfrey in Rosemary Gladstar's garden in East Barre, Vermont.

the path of the herb gardener

What is it that inspires a passion for herb gardening? For us, growing herbs is a natural expression of the strong spiritual connection we feel to the earth. We've found that gardening, a source of enjoyment for many, is a more intense experience for herbalists. It is our joy, our avocation, and our livelihood.

Herbalists have a great respect for the healing power of herbs, and so their relationship with the plants may be somewhat different from that of a household gardener with perennial beds or a vegetable patch. Herbalists meditate and dream about their herbs. They pray over herbs as they plant them and give thanks when they harvest them. They pour forth blessings into the food and medicine they prepare with their herbs because when they offer these prepared gifts, herbalists understand that the herbs affect not just the physical body of the recipient, but also the soul and the spirit.

◁ Herbalists often walk the path less taken but find it lined with bright and beautiful friends — in this case, tawny daylilies.

We are blessed in that we love the life we have chosen. We are both doing work that we find fulfilling and rewarding. The hours are long, but that doesn't seem to matter — so much of what we do seems more like play than work. We have both, at various times in our lives, held jobs that were less than fulfilling, where we watched the clock until quitting time. Now, instead, we often resent nightfall, the closing in of darkness, because it takes us away from our passion.

There was a time, however, when we began to grow weary of our garden work. Having our gardens open to the public felt like living in a fishbowl. The thousands of little details that must be attended to for a small business to be successful were becoming a grind. There was too much paperwork and never enough time to do it. We were forgetting the reasons why we had chosen to live our lives as gardeners and caretakers of a piece of land. We had lost a connection to our mission.

We were fortunate at that time to hear Paul Strauss, a well-respected herb farmer, give a lecture at the International Herb Symposium, a medicinal herb conference held in eastern Massachusetts every other year. The first words he said were all we needed to help us find our center again: "For a rich life, marry a piece of land."

For a rich life, marry a piece of land. Even today, several years later, we both vividly recall those words. What does it mean to marry a piece of land? For us, it means establishing an intimate relationship: putting our hands into the dirt, feeling it, rubbing it between our fingers,

smelling the richness of it; it means really getting to know our corner of the earth — its nuances, its beauty, even its uncomely side. It means commitment and responsibility.

When you marry a piece of land, you become so merged with it that you feel the earth's energy rising in spring. You hear the excitement in the bulbs as their first greenery breaks through the ground. You feel refreshed when parched soil receives the blessing of rain, and you feel the boggy weight when it becomes drenched in wetness.

Despite all the wide and varied differences that human beings around the world embody, we are in truth more alike than dissimilar. In the core of our being, we yearn to be connected to something real, something substantial, something to believe in — something larger than ourselves. We want to belong, to be a part of something that will endure beyond our short lives.

We are born within nations, artificial boundaries of land that give us a connection with the humanity within those borders. Many of us belong to a formal religion that connects us spiritually to wise men and women who have pondered life's meaning before us. We form family bonds and meaningful friendships that become an emotional and physical support circle. But when we link ourselves to a piece of land and commit ourselves to working with and really getting to know this piece of land, we become connected to the earth, to nature, to the great circle of life and death that governs all our days and endeavors.

△ Every day we bear witness to the little miracles in the garden. That we love the life we have chosen is evident in the joy we find in our daily life, whether we are harvesting flowers from angelica, as Shatoiya is doing here, making medicines from herbs grown in our garden, or simply getting down on our knees to weed. It is a blessing to interact with the cycles of life as part of our daily routine.

As we watch the seasons march through our gardens, we observe the process of life itself. Conception, birth, growth, and death: We can, like our ancient ancestors, become intimately acquainted with the cyclical nature of life.

Survival for early humans was tied to their profound knowledge of changeable Nature. Without the distractions and artificial conveniences of the modern world, our predecessors observed the world around them and knew Nature for what it was: a dispassionate arbiter and provider.

Modern life has separated us from this connection. We live in air-conditioned and heated homes, work in closed office buildings, drive in our cars to and from home, work, and play. We live in a sterile, artificial environment that neither bends nor bows to the cycles and calls of Nature. We are removed from the earth and, as such, removed from our truest roots.

We've had adult students who as children were never allowed to get dirty. These students were hesitant and timid on the first day of digging in the garden, but by the end of the nine-month program they gladly had dirt under their fingernails and dirty knees. Many of them were inspired to create their first herb garden at home and proudly brought scrapbooks with pictures showing their masterpiece from start to finish. These once dirt-wary students had "gotten it"; they had made a connection to the greater cycle of life.

◁ Respected educator and ethnobotanist James Duke strolls barefoot in his garden.

Pictured on pages 6–7: Cultivating diversity in the garden helps us appreciate diversity in the rest of our lives. Here, the showy globed flowers of giant allium frame a bushy stand of lavender.

For too long our culture has dishonored the creation. North America as we know it today was built by rough-hewn men and hardy women hacking at the wilderness, marching across the continent to realize our "Manifest Destiny." Woe to anything that stood in the way of progress, be it untamed wilderness, native cultures, or the vast supply of natural resources and scenic treasures that North America was blessed with.

Western culture has conquered this land from the Atlantic to the Pacific. We have subjugated all that once was wild. We are using up our treasure trove of natural resources at an alarming rate. We are killing what may be some of our greatest healers and teachers.

Rosemary Gladstar often calls plants "little green teachers." Once, while visiting our farm, she gave an interview to a reporter. She was talking about how much she has learned from the plants, how she considers them her most important teachers. The reporter, a little confused by these comments, asked, "What could you possibly learn from a tree?"

Rosemary looked the reporter in the eye and said, very matter-of-factly, "Patience."

The reporter looked as if she had been hit by a bolt of lightning. You could see the proverbial lightbulbs turning on throughout her consciousness.

For many people, spirituality and philosophy come from books and lectures, not nature. Trees and shrubs and flowers can't talk, so how could they possibly teach us anything? Western culture has spent so much energy over the last millennium trying to achieve mastery over nature that we have forgotten the lessons available therein. In an era in which we have explored most of the earth and seemingly conquered the wild frontiers, we have walked heedlessly straight past those who can teach us to live in this new world: the plants.

We live in an age of miracles. Much of what is commonplace today was impossible just a few years ago. Man-made wonders surround us. Modern science has created sensational technologies to astound us. In the movies and on television, we see increasingly fantastic and previously unimaginable phenomena on the screen. This proliferation of modern marvels has caused many of us to become jaded — desensitized — to the little miracles of life around us. How often do we notice and appreciate the Herculean effort put forth by the little dandelion that sprouts through a crack in the sidewalk? How wonderful to have the opportunity to experience a miracle like that.

Gardeners understand the miraculous. They surround themselves with little miracles every day, close at hand, in their gardens and in their homes. They plant seeds, add a little water, and then experience the joy and wonder of watching this seemingly alchemical combination sprout into rows (or pots or beds) of herbs and vegetables and flowers.

In the past, we worked for the survival of our children and their children and many more generations to come by building a strong nation that was able to defend itself against almost any threat. Now we must demonstrate our concern and obligation to those who will follow us by ensuring that there will be resources left to provide for them.

The Rosa mundi rose

We can do this by honoring the earth and the creation. Gardening is a simple and constructive way of doing this. If we can grow our medicines, if we grow our foods and seasonings, if we as individuals become more independent, we help our culture become more self-sufficient and in the process more sustainable.

Change is slow, yet inevitable. It's one of nature's many lessons. Let us do all that we can to effect positive, life-affirming changes for ourselves, our children, and our planet.

You as an individual can start effecting change by marrying a piece of land and taking responsibility for it. Care for it. Work with it. Love it. By doing these things you are making a change for the better. If enough individuals take steps like this, ripples of inspiration will spread outward, from individuals to communities to nations, as everywhere people strive to improve their own little corner of our earth.

Children recognize the miracles of gardening. Our friend Donna Sharp, an herbalist who sometimes teaches at our farm, is also an elementary school teacher in the inner city of Sacramento, California. She has made an impact on her community by starting an organic garden on the school grounds. A part of the garden is reserved for the children as a lab for their science class.

The children of the school love the garden. They can't wait to get outside to weed and plant. A severe punishment for

△ Silver lamb's ears, pink chive blossoms, and 'Johnson blue' geranium make a stunning array in this little border.

unruly behavior is not to be allowed to garden. The benefits the children receive from the garden are numerous. Not only do they get to work in the dirt and sunshine and learn about compost and worms, but they also earn the joy of sharing the fruits of their labor. The vegetables they harvest are proudly donated to local families in need. Our farm buys their herbs, and the money the students earn goes toward buying seed and supplies.

Donna shared with us a conversation she had with a few of her fourth- and fifth-graders as they lingered in the garden one afternoon. One child asked, "Miss Sharp, what happens to our bodies when we die?" Donna explained to them about burial and cremation. Another child asked, "If I died, could my ashes be put in this garden?" "Yes," replied one child quickly, "and when your ashes are put in this ground, you will become part of the dirt. And then you will be in each of the plants. And when they make tomatoes, people will eat you and then you will be a part of everything."

The cycle of life that gardens portray so beautifully can heal us as we are living and comfort us as we die. We have a friend in her forties who has dealt with three different cancers through her lifetime. What has kept her going is her love for her family, their love for her, and her joy in gardening. She will be moving into a brand-new home with a bare backyard, an empty palette for her to fill. She is excited by this chance to grow her dream herb garden. The excitement of this opportunity to co-create with the earth enlivens her, even if — especially if — it is the last thing she will ever do. The gift of a green legacy will be hers. Such is the power of the plants.

"It is only in the creation that all our ideas and conceptions of a word of God can unite. The creation speaketh a universal language, independently of human speech or human languages, multiplied and various as they be. It is an ever-existing original which every man can read. It cannot be forged; it cannot be counterfeited; it cannot be lost; it cannot be altered; it cannot be suppressed. It does not depend upon the will of man whether it shall be published or not; it publishes itself from one end of the earth to the other. It preaches to all nations and to all worlds; and this word of God reveals to man all that is necessary for man to know of God."

— Thomas Paine, "The Age of Reason" (1791)

△ A well-loved garden brings to light the story of its gardener and leaves a legacy to inspire future generations.

a garden to serve the community

We are the owners of Dry Creek Herb Farm & Learning Center, a refuge for herb lovers tucked in the foothills of the Sierras in Auburn, California. The farm has gardens open to the public as well as a gift shop, an apothecary, and indoor and outdoor classrooms. Shatoiya is an author, teacher, and herb and flower essence consultant. Richard has a degree in forestry and lends his expertise to the Learning Center's wilderness classes and mountain hikes. Together, working in conjunction with guest teachers, we teach the farm's extensive herbal apprenticeship programs.

◁ The small, narrow entrance walkway is the perfect intimate introduction to the farm. The curving path was designed so that every few steps into the garden offers a completely new view. We hoped this would slow down visitors and help them relax into the leisurely pace of the farm.

When Shatoiya first moved to Auburn, Dry Creek Herb Farm was no more than a twinkle in her eye. Since she was renting the land, she considered container gardening. Two weeks after arriving, though, she had a strange experience. She was sitting in her living room when suddenly she was moved — as if someone had pulled her by the front of the shirt — to go outside. She felt herself guided around the perimeter of the farm, then led in a spiral closing toward the center. Shatoiya understood. This was a promise of a sacred trust, of a marriage to the land. The transformation waiting to happen here became clear to her, and she decided to start planting in the ground the next day.

The first big challenge was the land. Much of it was rocky, and what soil existed was clay. Many areas were filled with stubborn Bermuda grass, and since Shatoiya wanted to garden organically, herbicides were out of the question. In addition, Shatoiya had brought fifty beloved plants with her from a previous farm in Ventura County, and they needed to get into the ground quickly.

The ground that was most immediately workable was a small plot, 30 feet by 20 feet, that had been the previous tenant's goat pen. With the help of friends, Shatoiya constructed two raised beds, each 6 feet by 20 feet, using 18-inch redwood boards. She bought a combination of topsoil and mushroom compost to fill them. Old Italian tiles found in one of the sheds on the property became the decorative walkway between the beds.

Shatoiya then planted her old herb friends, and the culinary and fragrance garden was born. Years later, the culinaries were moved to their own bed, and the original two beds became the fragrance garden.

This was the only garden for the first two years. As it grew and flourished, Shatoiya concentrated on improving the rest of the grounds. She painstakingly pulled out the Bermuda grass by hand, year after year, until she could plant in a "weed-free" zone. She cleaned her neighbor's chicken coop and horse stalls in exchange for their beneficial manure. She lavished this on any area that had topsoil. On the areas that didn't, she constructed raised beds.

As a single businesswoman, Shatoiya had to be conservative with her funds. She did much of the construction with recycled materials and remnants from various friends' projects. Stones from land being graded, railroad ties, pallets — all became part of the gardens. The back of the farm was abundant with large serpentine rocks, and those were moved into circles to form planting beds. Shatoiya traded homemade herbal salves and teas for help with the labor.

▷ With four friends, two pickup trucks, and ten trips to an abandoned road project, we managed to collect and stack enough stone to build an inexpensive raised bed. A student built the hops trellis in the background; he traded his carpentry skills for herb classes.

Two years after starting that first garden, Shatoiya drove to San Francisco to attend a conference. En route, an out-of-control vehicle spun around in front of her, causing a minor traffic pileup and denting the fender on Shatoiya's pickup. Nevertheless, she went on to the conference; later she filed an insurance claim.

A short time later a representative from the insurance company came to her farm to discuss her claim. She noted that as he entered the house he removed his shoes, in accordance with a small sign on the door. She thought it looked odd, this man in coat and tie in his stocking feet, but that small act of politeness impressed her.

During the course of the interview they came across a number of things they shared in common, notably a love of nature. Well, of course, that insurance man was Richard, and after two years of joyful courtship they were married. A couple of years later Richard quit his job so they could work together on the gardens.

Eventually we were able to buy the land that has become Dry Creek Herb Farm. Each year we've planted a new garden or built some project: a bench, a pond, a classroom. And we continue to compost and work the unused land, preparing it for future gardens. On our two and a half acres we now have ten theme gardens, three ponds, a nursery, two classrooms, a cabin for overnight students, an herb-drying shed, a chicken coop, a llama pen, and a thriving herb shop.

◁ Richard, with an armload of vegetables, passes by a signpost pointing the way to all of Dry Creek Herb Farm's attractions.

"I've always had a strong connection to nature. When I first saw Shatoiya's garden, I saw a place where natural forces were honored and allowed their own expression."

— Richard de la Tour

Shatoiya and Richard de la Tour's Dry Creek Herb Farm

GARDEN FEATURES

A Roses

B Daylilies

C Bulbs and flowers

D Garden arbor

E Rosemary planted over the septic system

F Privacy hedge

G Pond

H Rock garden

I Women's garden

J Grapes

K Fragrance gardens

L Flower garden

M Working garden

N Moon garden

O Medicine-wheel garden

P Rose garden

Q Storage

R Drying room

S Medicine key

T Dyers garden

U Children's garden

V Barn

W Yurt

X Sweat lodge

Y Fire pit

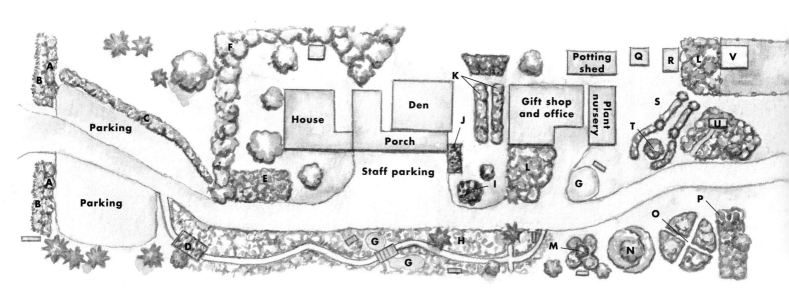

Lamb's ear lines the path over the garden pond.

Jerusalem artichoke grows side by side with several varieties of yarrow in the children's garden.

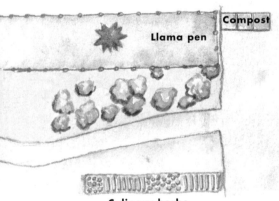

Culinary herbs

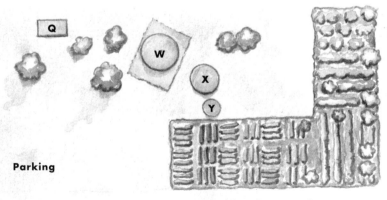

Vegetables, fruits, and nuts

Everything is connected. However you try to change an environment, however much you think you can control it, nature will have her say. As our land became greener and wetter, it also became more attractive to snails. In our third year they became our biggest problem, and they continued to be for the next two years.

We tried all the natural snail treatments we'd heard of, with little success. We set out pans of beer in the garden and harvested the drowned snails. The pans would collect maybe half a dozen snails a day, which wasn't enough. Sometimes we wouldn't get any snails because our dog drank the beer! And even cheap beer was prohibitively expensive over a long haul.

We put out boards on small legs in the garden to encourage snails to collect under them during the heat of the day. Again, this netted only a few snails, and we could see hundreds of them in the evening crossing our walkways. We put copper strips on the legs of tables that held small potted plants for sale. This kept the snails off the tables, but the garden plants were still at their mercy.

One of the most successful treatments we found was to offer local children a penny for each snail they collected. This worked successfully until the children became more enterprising and priced themselves out of the market. We had one young man who couldn't bring himself to salt the snails, so he set them free across the street. We are still hoping that our neighbors didn't see him!

The snail problem was exasperating. There were many herbs we couldn't grow because the snails ate them as soon as we put them in the ground. Entire echinacea plants, for example, would disappear completely overnight!

Now for the good news. We have finally discovered an organic method for completely eliminating your snail population. The bad news is that it's a method not available to everyone: chickens.

We originally purchased our chickens for their eggs and for their contribution to the compost pile. We started with fewer than a dozen. Within a few weeks in the garden, to our surprise the chickens had just about wiped out the snail population

We now keep two roosters and fifteen hens and find that to be a reasonable ratio. Any more roosters than that and fights break out. We've gathered quite a variety. We have a number of silkies, which have "fuzzy"-looking feathers and were described by one young visitor as looking like two-legged poodles. We also have Polish Crested chickens, which are known for their unusual head feathers and look quite regal.

We enjoy having chickens on our land. They have an entertaining and humorous social culture. During mating rituals, for example, you can almost hear the strutting roosters calling out, "Hey, baby, what's your sign?" And all the chickens come down from their coop to our house to wake us up in the morning; they raise a chorus of cackles if we try to sleep late.

The disadvantage of having chickens is that they can destroy baby plants. We use chicken wire to fence off young plants for their first one to two months. When we remove the wire, the chickens scratch around the mature plants but generally do not kill them. Occasionally

△ Goldie, one of our chickens, passes by our hand-painted wagon, which we use as both a garden tool and a garden ornament.

we lose some plants to chickens, but only a fraction of the number we lost to the snails.

There's another slight disadvantage: Where we used to step on snails if we didn't watch where we walked, now we occasionally step in something altogether different, a little "gift" from the chick-ens. And chickens do make noise — in a setting less rural than ours, they might bother the neighbors. If you decide you'd like to share your land with chickens, our advice is to check the local bylaws first. Some city or town ordinances allow chickens but not roosters, and some, we're sure, do not allow chickens at all.

Pictured on pages 22–23: This corner of our English Garden combines the bright yellow of calendula, pansies, and geraniums with the deep purple of borage and violets.

We have many blessings here at our farm: Wonderful herbalists and spiritual teachers come from around the world to share their knowledge; various groups, from small children to elders, visit us regularly; and we've had all kinds of support from our customers, students, and community. After twelve years of giving students in our gardening classes cuttings from our plants to take home, we know we are now a part of thousands of herb gardens. And as those gardeners share *their* cuttings, we marvel at the thought of so many green havens.

As our garden grew and prospered, we came to realize that it has a life of its own and its own vision of what it wants to be. We must confess that our original vision was for a private garden, open only to students. But as time went on, our gardens became a meeting place for our community, and our little store is the local apothecary.

Throughout the year we sponsor a number of events: an Easter egg hunt, a Mother's Day celebration, and a winter holiday open house. We've had many local residents tell us how much they look

▽ The bounty of our garden is made manifest in our gift shop, where we sell dried herbs, teas, and other botanical treasures.

forward to these events. Several clubs and organizations, from the local chamber of commerce to the California Native Plant Society, hold meetings here, savoring such a forum in this lovely garden setting. And we have annual visits from public and private schools and homeschoolers.

To accommodate our garden's inclination to be more public, we have tried to make the gardens even more inviting.

Despite poor soil, we've added trees where we could to increase shade (temperatures are often in the 90s or above in the summer). We've set out seats and built arbor-covered benches to encourage visitors to sit and take in the garden. Picnic tables allow guests to bring sack lunches. And the llamas, chickens, cats, and dogs give families a real sense of visiting a country setting.

▽ By midsummer, the hops vines blanket the top of this arbor, making it a shady spot to sit to escape the hot California sun.

"Shatoiya's gardens are an inspiration to me. I love their whimsical nature, playfulness, and rich abundance, and I admire her perseverance in creating such beauty in an area of packed soil, rock, and sparse water."

— *Rosemary Gladstar*

There are many joys and challenges in owning a public garden. People who seek out public gardens are some of the most beautiful people around; they have a connection to nature and an appreciation for things natural. We have met some of the most interesting people you can imagine. Opening our gardens to the public has been rewarding and helps confirm our purpose in life. We admit we are sentimental and find it moving to watch a child's joy upon discovering that it's okay to roll in the chamomile bed, or to see romance rekindled by a couple strolling hand in hand along our garden paths. It is immensely gratifying to have strangers tell us, time and time again, how beautiful they think our gardens are.

On the other hand, there are some challenges in making your gardens an accessible attraction. One of the lessons we have learned from owning a public garden, and from our conversations with other public gardeners, is that if the community considers you a public garden, some of them will assume that you are open all the time.

For example, one Valentine's Day we were planning a romantic candlelight dinner for two in the gardens, after hours. A table was set with a tablecloth, wine, and a wondrous gourmet meal, ready for romantic glances over the glow of flickering candles. The perfect evening was at hand.

Just as we popped the cork on a bottle of fine California wine, a young man came up the driveway. "I saw that your sign said you were closed, but I know you won't mind if I just wander the gardens." We said that yes, we did mind, and would he please come back when we were open to the public. He assumed a look of incredulity, but he left.

We've come home to find that people have opened our front gate and are wandering around. We've had people drive over our neighbor's lawn to see into our gardens while we were closed. We've had countless people tell us they drove for hours, some even for days, to see our gardens, without even considering calling ahead to find out what hours we were open.

This continues to be a big issue for us and for others we know who have made their farms and gardens public. To turn away someone who is seeking inspiration, an earth connection, fresh vegetables, or herb medicine is extremely difficult. We all appreciate the support of our customers and their desire to experience the green energy, but we also need to have a life outside of the public domain.

◁ △ Funded by a grant from the Herb Growing & Marketing Network, the children's garden has become a well-loved gathering place for little ones and a "green baby-sitter" for parents who wish to shop in peace in our herb store. We built raised beds in a giant star shape and filled them with herbs from Shatoiya's *The Herbalist of Yarrow*, a fairy tale of plant wisdom, so children could meet the herbs they read about. One of the favorite attractions is a raised bed of aromatic chamomile and soft lamb's ears, perfect for rolling around on. A colorful play-house and turtle habitat inspire imagination and play.

At first we were open seven days a week, and because we were working feverishly to get our business running, that wasn't a problem. As the business became more established, we were able to take a little time off for ourselves. But if we wanted private time, peace, and quiet, we had to leave home. It was frustrating to live in these beautiful gardens and not be able to go out and enjoy them.

On a drive home from a visit with family for the holidays, we had a long discussion about what we wanted to do with our lives. We were working too hard. We had created the image of living with the seasons in a natural way, of working with nature to provide for our needs, but we weren't really living that way. We weren't walking our talk.

We decided that success was more about seeking the lifestyle we wanted and not so much about making a few dollars. We decided to close the farm to the public on weekdays so that we could concentrate on the things we enjoyed doing: teaching and working in the garden. At first there was some resistance from the staff and some of our customers, but in the long run the business has become more rewarding, both for us and for them.

ASTROLOGY GARDENS

Nicholas Culpeper was an English physician-astrologer of the early seventeenth century. He is most known for his herbal formulas and his works linking astrology and herbs. Astrology gardens are a part of many old European gardens. They are generally planted in a circle, each herb covering a twelfth of the astrological wheel. We've offered a few suggestions here, but we highly recommend that you read Culpeper's work yourself to decide which herbs are best for your garden.

Zodiac Sign	Governance	Related Herb
Aries	Rules the head	Wood betony
Taurus	Rules the throat	Marsh mallow root
Gemini	Rules the nervous system	Lavender
Cancer	Rules the stomach	Lemon balm
Leo	Rules the heart	Borage
Virgo	Rules the intestines	Mint
Libra	Rules the kidneys	Parsley
Scorpio	Rules the reproductive system	Nettle
Sagittarius	Rules the liver	Dandelion
Capricorn	Rules the skeletal system	Horsetail
Aquarius	Rules the circulatory system	Rosemary
Pisces	Rules the feet	Chamomile

△ Our medicine-wheel garden is hung with prayer ribbons, each representing the prayer of one of our students. Following traditional custom, the ribbons are hung on the wheel each spring equinox, then burned on the winter solstice. Along the circumference of the garden, herbs express the classic astrological associations developed by Nicholas Culpeper.

Our garden is full of wonderful memories. We were married in Grand Teton National Park in Wyoming but came home to a wonderful reception in the garden with friends, dancers, musicians, and an incredible feast. And our gardens have hosted numerous wedding ceremonies, reunions, and community gatherings. But the times we most treasure are when it is just the two of us. We love to stroll hand in hand after hours listening to the sounds of the garden: the light tinkling of wind chimes, the gentle clucking of the chickens, the pleasant trickle of water flowing in the ponds, the coos and whistles from wild birds, and the soft whinny of our neighbor's horse.

Evenings are also the time for reflection on the blessings of each day: teachings shared in class, stories of herbal healings from customers, herbs that were harvested, and those that will be ready to harvest tomorrow. In these quiet times, we harvest the true fruits of our labor.

Our staff like to tease us about the fact that we still act like honeymooners after several years of married life; they call us "schmoopies" and feign nausea at our romantic glances. We attribute our ability to hang on to the romance of our relationship, at least in part, to our connection to the earth. Because we share a passion for the little miracles that happen all around us in the garden, we appreciate the miracle that is our love for each other. We hope and expect that gardening will help keep us healthy, vigorous, and passionate for a long, long time.

◁ Early summer in the English garden displays a variety of textures and colors.

Wisdom from the garden

"We've been inspired by many people, including Louis and Virginia Saso and Rosemary Gladstar. But our most profound inspiration has always been the land we live on."

— *Shatoiya de la Tour*

▷ In the moon garden, a coyote howls at the various moon mobiles hanging from the catalpa tree. Stones edge the full moon circle and the crescent shape of the quarter moon, which we've planted with silvery, strong-scented artemisias. Artemisia is associated with Artemis, the hunting goddess of the woods and of the quarter moon. In time, these ghostly plants will spread and fill the outer crescent, creating a graphic display of the quarter moon.

Our Favorite Herbs

"The first herb I ever dreamed of was dandelion. It has been a powerful teacher for me ever since then. Dandelions are a metaphor for herbal healers in this country: The more you try to weed them out, the more they spring up; they are humble and gentle, yet very effective, and they support the body's natural ability to heal."

— Shatoiya de la Tour

We've chosen dandelion, borage, and angelica as our favorite herbs to feature in this book. As you'll see in the following pages, these wonderful plants offer both beauty and medicinal potency. As we've grown and used them, we've come to love them, and we hope you will, too.

Dandelion

To the horror of many suburbanites, we like the sight of shaggy golden flowers poking out of a green, grassy lawn. If eventually dandelions take over the lawn, so much the better! This humble weed is so helpful to human health that it sprouts up everywhere trying to call attention to itself. Imagine the tenacity it takes to grow up out of a crack in the sidewalk!

Traditional Medicinal Uses

This gentle but effective herb is a powerhouse of nutrition and medicine. One-half cup of dandelion greens contains 122 percent of the U.S. recommended daily allowance of vitamin A, 15 percent of vitamin C, 7 percent of calcium, and 5 percent of iron. It also contains potassium, thiamine, riboflavin, and other trace minerals. All this and only 19 calories!

For those taking diuretics, potassium loss is a major concern. Dandelion leaves are naturally diuretic and also high in potassium, so they are a great natural and safe alternative. Dandelion root is great food for the kidneys and liver, helping to keep these major organs of elimination and filtration in optimum health.

Other uses for the leaf and root of dandelion include, but are not limited to, kidney and liver ailments, constipation, kidney stones, poor digestion, gout, arthritis, water retention, poor skin, menstrual and prostate problems, and imbalanced blood sugar. Dandelion root is also often used as a coffee substitute.

Growing and Harvesting

Planted in a garden with rich soil, dandelion leaves will grow 8 to 12 inches long, and the flowers become big golden globes. Sow seeds in autumn or after the last frost. In mild climates, seeds sown in early fall may sprout to offer winter greens. Since this herb will grow anywhere, under any conditions, it's hard to go wrong.

For optimum taste, many books will tell you to harvest leaves for cooking before the flowers appear. However, we have gathered the leaves throughout the growing seasons and have found them delicious. We use the pre-flower leaves fresh for salads and the later leaves for steaming or adding to casseroles.

The root can be harvested in its second fall. Fresh, it can be added to stir-fries. We usually chop it and dry it for medicinal use.

Harvest the flowers when they are in their fullness. Whole flowers are delicious when sautéed in butter. Fastidious types will insist that you pull the petals off the sepal and chop off the minute bit of white at the end of each petal. They say this small bitter part will tarnish the flavor of your dandelion wine, scones, cakes, or whatever you are using the petals for. We think life is too short for such antics and would rather spend our time drinking the dandelion wine.

DANDELION *TARAXACUM OFFICINALE*
Plant Cycle: Perennial, Zones 3–11
Propagation: Dandelion is easily started from seed.
Parts Used: Flower, leaf, root

Borage

When in its fullness, with its glorious, large oval leaves and blue, starlike flowers, borage is the most-often-asked-about plant at our farm. It has a reputation for "gladdening the heart" and seems to speak to people on some primal level. Easy to grow, and constantly reseeding itself until the dead of winter, this herb is a must for every garden.

Traditional Medicinal Uses

Borage is known for its calcium content, which is easily accessible to the body when the herb is tinctured in vinegar or made into a tea. We include borage in our circulatory formulas because of its joyous affinity with the heart. It is also a mild adrenal tonic.

Borage seed oil is sold as a supplement because it contains gamma linoleic acid (GLA), an important nutrient. A deficiency in GLA has been linked to numerous health problems.

A LIGHT-HEARTED TEA

1 part dried borage leaf and flower
1 part dried wild oat tops
1 part dried lemon balm leaf
½ part dried red raspberry leaf
½ part dried linden leaf and flower
½ part dried chamomile
½ part dried lemon verbena leaves

Blend ingredients and store in a tightly covered glass container away from heat and light. Measure 1 scant teaspoon of herb blend per cup of water. Bring the water to a boil, pour over the herbs, cover, and let steep 10 to 15 minutes. Strain before serving.

Growing and Harvesting

We planted a few borage seeds eleven years ago and have never had to sow seeds again: We have borage everywhere! However, we don't consider it a pest. The single large taproot is easy to pull up if it sprouts where it isn't wanted. Feed these thinned-out plants to any of your livestock, or toss them in your compost pile, where they'll act as accelerators.

Borage can grow to be 3 feet high and 3 feet wide. It isn't picky about soil, although rich loam makes for bigger plants. Because of the thinness and openness of its leaves, it likes lots of water. If the leaves start to droop or curl in the summer, you need to water them more.

Borage flowers at first are a beautiful shade of blue. Once pollinated by bees, however, they turn purple, then pink. Bees don't see pink very well, so it's as if the well-pollinated flowers are saying, "Oh, no, not tonight, I have a headache!"

The flowers are edible — we pick them right off their stems, pull off their fuzzy sepals, and toss them with greens and other edible flowers for a delicious, colorful, and healthful salad.

To harvest the leaves, wait until they are relatively large and mature, then cut them a half inch or so from the main stalk. The large central stalk is hollow, so you want to be careful not to cut into it, as that may cause the plant to rot and die.

We use the leaves for tea. We wonder about herb books that suggest using the leaves fresh in salad. These authors must be armchair herbalists who have never felt the hairy, prickly leaves — they're definitely not for fresh consumption!

BORAGE *BORAGO OFFICINALIS*
Plant Cycle: Annual
Propagation: Borage is easily started from seed.
Parts Used: Flower, leaf

Angelica

Angelica is a graceful plant all season long, but when in bloom it's a show-stopper. Three-foot-high stalks, some of them 3 inches in diameter, support the large compound green leaves that form a broad basal rosette. From their center sprout stems that rise 2 to 3 feet above the circle of leaves and support the huge, umbrella-like clusters of light green to cream-colored flowers.

Traditional Medicinal Uses

Angelica root has a specific affinity with the bronchial tubes. We have seen people with bronchitis go through a 1-ounce bottle of tincture in a few days and be healed of this condition. Angelica root is often used in combination with other herbs in teas for severe colds and coughs. It is also a liver tonic, and it is one of several ingredients used to create herbal bitters.

The seeds can be chewed and ingested much like fennel seeds, as an after-dinner digestive (two to six seeds should be sufficient). They have also been used to assuage the nausea that often accompanies the flu.

Caution: Angelica can increase bleeding during menstruation and should be avoided just before and during the cycle by women with a tendency toward heavy menstrual flow.

Growing and Harvesting

Angelica is a biennial. It's best to purchase first-year plants from a nursery, as seed propagation is iffy. However, if angelica feels you have made a good home for her, she will grace you by self-seeding after her second-year bloom. From a plant that develops hundreds of seeds, you may get anywhere from two to thirty new plants the following spring.

The root of angelica is what's most often used medicinally, and it should be harvested in the first fall. However, by harvesting the root you have taken the life of the plant, and you miss out on the fantastic bloom the next year. Grow several angelica plants so you can harvest roots of some in the fall and leave others to bloom the next spring.

Angelica leaves can be used in small amounts for cooking when you want an accent flavor similar to lovage or a sharp parsley. In Victorian times, the stems were chopped and boiled in sugar, then laid out to dry. This candy is still a gourmet treat in parts of England and France.

A BITTER TONIC

In many herbal traditions, the digestive system is considered the center of health. We receive much *chi* (energy) from our food when it is properly digested. Bitter tonics are alcoholic extracts of herbs that are *carminatives* — they aid digestion. Many people find they have more energy and feel more lively when they make bitters a regular part of their diet.

2 parts dried dandelion root	1 part dried chamomile flowers
2 parts dried gentian root	1 part dried fennel seeds
1 part dried angelica root	Brandy

Blend the herbs. Fill a small jar about two-thirds full with the herbal blend, then fill the jar to the top with a good-quality brandy. Place wax paper between the jar top and the lid and close tightly. Give the jar a good shake daily. After two or three days, top off with more brandy. After two weeks, strain the extract through a cloth to remove the herbs. Squeeze the herbs to get out all the liquid, then toss the spent herbs in the compost. Store your extract in a glass jar away from heat and light.

To use these bitters, take 2 droppersful under the tongue first thing in the morning, at least 15 minutes before eating. They can also be taken as needed to help stave off sugar cravings.

Caution: These bitters should not be used by women who are pregnant or who are prone to heavy menstrual flow.

ANGELICA *ANGELICA ARCHANGELICA*
Plant Cycle: Biennial, Zones 4–9
Propagation: The seeds lose their viability rather quickly, so we recommend buying a small seedling from a nursery.
Parts Used: Root, leaf

the wild woman's garden

Rosemary Gladstar of East Barre, Vermont, has been a role model and an inspiration for a generation of herbalists, as well as a driving force in herbal education. Many believe that she has done more to promote the spread of herbalism than anyone else in North America. She founded the California School of Herbal Studies in 1976; she is responsible for many herb symposiums held each year around the world; she is the founder and formulator of several herb-products companies; and she is a prolific and well-respected author. Rosemary is also the visionary behind United Plant Savers, a nonprofit organization dedicated to saving endangered medicinal plants.

◁ In Rosemary Gladstar's wild garden, it is difficult to determine where the garden ends and the forest begins.

> *"My gardens have a
> carefree wildness to them.
> They blend with the
> native environment,
> flowing in and out of the
> natural landscape that
> surrounds them."*
>
> *— Rosemary Gladstar*

When you first meet Rosemary Gladstar, it is almost impossible not to notice the wild nature spirit that is her center. She has a knowing sparkle in her eye and boundless enthusiasm. Few people can match her energy stride for stride or equal her passion for life.

In the wild northern forest, Rosemary has carved out an herbalist's garden that is both civilized and wild. In fact, the casual observer might have difficulty discerning where the cultivated garden ends and the wild forest begins. Rosemary treasures the frontier between the cultivated garden and the wild land surrounding it. This band where wild and domestic plants coexist displays a rich abundance and exceptional variety. Rosemary loves to witness the merging of nature and civilization and observe how they affect each other.

As an herbalist and a gardener, Rosemary is always aware of the tenuous thread by which a number of our native medicinal plants cling to their existence. She is greatly concerned with preserving our botanical heritage, and her garden includes as many endangered plants as space and climate will allow. In addition, Rosemary is one of the founders of United Plant Savers, an organization dedicated to the preservation of botanical diversity and the protection of endangered plant treasures.

▷ Subtle and narrow walkways in the garden give visitors the feeling of being explorers on a wild forest path.

Twelve years ago, Rosemary, a California native, found herself living on five hundred acres in the beautiful forests of northern Vermont, horrified at the prospect of gardening in a place where the growing season doesn't start until Memorial Day and usually ends around Labor Day. This land had not had a cultivated garden on it for as long as anyone could remember, and it was in a wild state. Growing here were some of Rosemary's favorite botanical friends, including blue cohosh, clintonia, dog's ear violet, and wild leek. Rosemary asked herself, "How could I do any better?" So for the first three growing seasons Rosemary's garden was sown and tended entirely by Mother Nature.

Finally, at the urging of her students, who desired some guidance in herb gardening, she put spade to soil and started creating her "civilized" garden. She and her students turned the soil and laid out a medicine-wheel garden. They offered tobacco, in the Native American tradition, as a blessing for the new garden.

Rosemary gave each student a kernel of blue corn from ears that had been given to her by Sun Bear, a Native American healer and the author of *The Medicine Wheel*. She also gave each student-gardener a plant to place with the kernel of blue corn in the medicine-wheel garden — wherever the students felt called to plant them.

The result was a beautiful garden laid out with the help of Mother Nature and the spirits who guided the students. To Rosemary's surprise, the kernels of blue corn sprouted as well, and she was doubly blessed. (Now, however, when Rosemary offers corn to bless her planting, she grinds it into meal first.)

Being a California girl, Rosemary had to rethink some of her gardening tricks. Although she now claims to have the skill to garden above the Arctic Circle, she had a bit of trouble getting started. First she put in some of her favorite Mediterranean plants. She happily watched them flourish until the first snow in October, when they withered away, never to be seen again.

Then Rosemary sought the advice of local experts Judith and Rachel Kane, owners of Perennial Pleasures Nursery in Hardwick, Vermont. After her first visit to Perennial Pleasures, Rosemary's worries were gone — she was relieved to know that her gardening days in Vermont were not over after all. Judith and Rachel helped Rosemary in her first tentative steps toward gardening in a Zone 3 climate.

Rosemary's gardening philosophy has always been to let nature have an important hand in the creation of the garden. Let nature dictate where the lines of the garden will be drawn. Let nature decide what plants will be in this garden, because it will be nature who ultimately determines the success or failure of the garden. When faced with tough gardening decisions, Rosemary always asks herself, "What would Mother Nature do?"

A gardener's mantra

Pictured on pages 46–47: The first thing you notice at Sage Mountain are the great terraced gardens. The stonework is an attractive and clever way to deal with the problem of creating gardens on sloping land.

◁ A brick mandala with a reflective Buddha as its centerpiece sets the tone for this meditation garden.

Two elders for whom Rosemary is particularly thankful are Adelma Grenier Simmons and Adele Dawson. Rosemary credits Adelma Simmons with starting the current renaissance of the American country herb garden. She has found great inspiration in Adelma's vision and the grand scope of her gardens at Caprilands (see page 193), famous for its flower-laden luncheons.

In Adele Dawson, Rosemary found both inspiration and friendship. When Rosemary took up residence in her current portion of heaven, she found herself blessed to have Adele as a neighbor, just over the hill. Adele, who recently passed on after almost one hundred years of walking this planet, was also a lover of wild and untamed gardens. People came from far and wide to visit this wise and generous woman and follow her about her free-form gardens. She grew all her own food and medicines and attributed her longevity in part to that.

Adele's gardens grow in the shadow of Vermont's highest waterfall. Shatoiya was with a small group of women whom Rosemary took to meet Adele and tour her gardens. The day was hot, and the waterfall was cool and beautiful. They were thankful that Adele didn't bat an eye when they asked if they could go for a dip. She understood the desire to be one with your surroundings!

When Adele visited Rosemary for the first time, she brought a slip of comfrey, which, of course, has now become a *field* of comfrey. For this Rosemary is eternally grateful, as comfrey has become one of her favorite herbs.

Rosemary once told us that she was inspired by our persistence in creating, despite difficult soil conditions, the beauty in our gardens at Dry Creek Herb Farm. She said that she especially enjoys our garden's whimsy and playfulness. We were honored. Rosemary has been a great inspiration to us, and to be able to return the favor is a wonderful blessing.

Rosemary has drawn inspiration from the many gardeners, herbalists, and spirits who have crossed her path, but the primary influence in her life is nature. Rosemary says it's important to enjoy the creativity a human might bring to a garden, but we must understand that the real artist is Mother Nature. Look around and see the work of nature in the mountains, forests, glades, moss-covered pools, and desert landscapes — truly, what mortal landscaper or gardener can compete with such beauty? Rosemary's connection to and love for Mother Nature is the single driving force in her life. She considers it her purpose to help people interact with nature, feel its inspiration, and reconnect and recommit to being caretakers of the earth.

A showy peony

▷ Because she is a wild spirit, Rosemary invites all sorts of enchanting beings to reside in her garden. If you look carefully about the gardens, you will see a number of "elf houses" built to attract fey residents.

Golden Seal
Hydrastis canadensis
One of our most prized woodland
medicinal plants, this herb is truly
'at risk' in its native habitats.
Parts used: organically cultivated
root and rhizome.

American ginseng

Goldenseal

One of the most rewarding experiences in Rosemary's life has been her participation in the creation of United Plant Savers, a nonprofit, grassroots organization dedicated to the conservation and cultivation of at-risk native medicinal plants.

When Rosemary moved to the Northeast, she looked forward to exploring the beautiful hardwood forests that have been home to many of the medicinal plant species that she came to know in her herbal practice. To her horror she discovered that many of these herbal allies were no longer plentiful in the wild and that some were even endangered, perilously close to extinction.

Rosemary started planting, often by herself, at-risk species in a five-hundred-acre preserve adjacent to her home in Vermont. United Plant Savers is now setting up a number of plant preserves across North America, as well as promoting responsible wildcrafting and encouraging herb gardeners to grow at-risk plants in their home gardens.

It seems that Rosemary never rests, never stops dreaming. She has recently, through tremendous effort and expense, saved a beautiful untamed portion of wilderness adjacent to her land. Hanna Hill Sanctuary, a hundred-acre home to deer, bear, moose, and numerous other forest creatures and native plants, is open to the many who wish to make a pilgrimage to this sacred land.

Rosemary has succeeded in preserving this land for eternity. Because of her reverence for the wild and her willingness to fight for it, she has given us a great legacy.

United Plant Savers can be reached at:

United Plant Savers
P.O. Box 98
East Barre, VT 05649

Phone: (802) 496-7053
Fax: (802) 496-9988
E-mail: info@plantsavers.org
Web site: www.plantsavers.org

◁ Rosemary is working hard to restore the forest medicinal-plant population. She has painstakingly replanted stands of ginseng, blue cohosh, and goldenseal and encouraged the spread of Solomon's seal and sarsaparilla. As these plantings mature, they will be harvested in a sustainable way.

"A gardener should always endeavor to create a garden space that invites friends to sit and inspires good conversation."

— *Shatoiya de la Tour*

◁ Comfortable chairs and a weatherworn but sturdy coffee table offer a quiet place to sit and enjoy good company in Rosemary's garden.

The Garden at Sage Mountain

GARDEN FEATURES

A Entrance garden, with native medicinal herbs and perennials

B Slate wall

C Foot trail to the yurt

D Slate wall edged on top with flowers

E Lawn for outdoor classroom

F Shade garden

G Woodland garden

H The "Grandfather Tree," a giant blue spruce

I Herb garden

J Natural twig arbor

K Driveway

L "Weeds Are Wonderful" medicinal weed garden

M Fairy castle garden

N Medicine-wheel garden

O Climbing vines, including hops, roses, and clematis

P Garden in the works

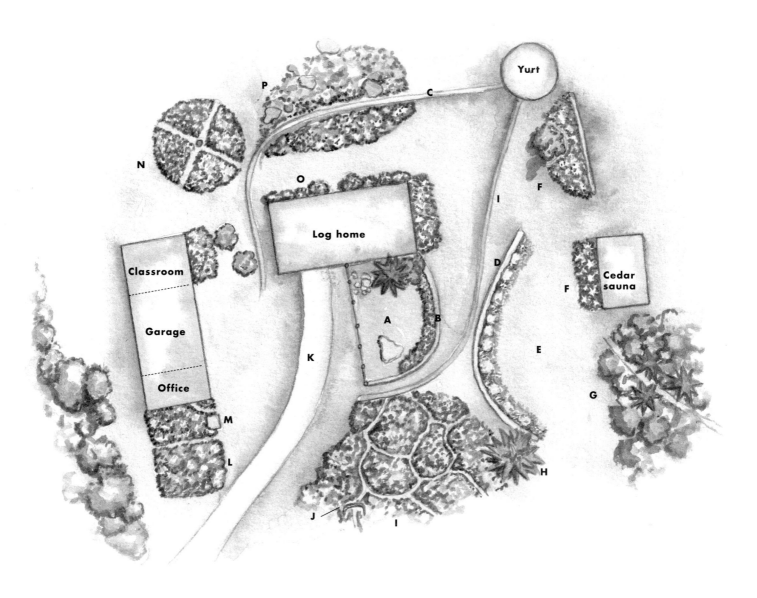

The foot trail leading to the yurt, bordered by ferns and maple trees

A fairy castle

Bright yellow whorled loosestrife marks the entrance garden at the front of Rosemary's log home.

Rosemary's outdoor classroom

A universal peace pole

Rosemary's Favorite Herbs

Rosemary selected comfrey, bee balm, and her namesake, rosemary, as her favorite herbs. Over the following pages you'll find information to help you get to know these wonders of the herb world.

Russian Comfrey

Comfrey is a favorite of many herbalists, both for its beauty in the garden and for its potent healing properties.

Traditional Medicinal Uses

Comfrey root and leaf are potent and effective healers. However, there has been some controversy over their safety. Some studies have shown that certain types of alkaloids found in comfrey can contribute to liver disease. However, the studies were using a synthetic version of these alkaloids, not the naturally occurring alkaloids found in comfrey. In addition, you'd have to eat enormous amounts of comfrey over your lifetime to ingest the dosages found harmful.

Comfrey is a sweet and soothing herb. Its mucilage is healing to mucous membranes, which means that it can work wonders on irritated tissues in our respiratory, digestive, and urinary systems. It is considered a primary herb for ulcers.

Comfrey is also a nutritive herb, with a high calcium and protein content that is a great tonic to the musculoskeletal system. According to wild-foods expert François Couplan, comfrey is unusual in that it contains all the essential amino acids and is therefore a complete protein.

Topically, comfrey can be used as a poultice or in a bath to soothe strained, sprained, or sore muscles and joints. It also can be used externally and internally to speed the healing of broken bones. Because it contains allantoin, the same constituent for which aloe vera is famed, comfrey is a common ingredient in healing skin salves.

Growing and Harvesting

The slightest piece of comfrey root will grow to be a big, beautiful plant. We have a water faucet surrounded by comfrey because once a student washed a root there and a small piece fell to the ground and took hold. Forewarned is forearmed. Grow this herb where its vigor can be controlled.

Comfrey isn't too picky about soil, but if you are growing it for the roots, you will want to give it soil that is loose, rich, and moist. Under the hot, dry sun of the California valleys and other desert climes, comfrey prefers partial shade, but most everywhere else it likes full sun.

Animals love comfrey — we feed it to our llamas, rabbits, goats, and dogs. Our chickens love it; if given the chance, they will eat it down to the ground.

Harvest the root in the early spring, just as the leaves are beginning to sprout, or in the fall. Although you may dig deep, we can almost guarantee you won't get the whole root. Wash off the dirt but not the nice brown skin. Toss the chopped fresh root into a stir-fry or dry the root for tea by slicing it into coin-shaped medallions and laying them on a screen.

The leaves can be cooked fresh, like spinach greens, or dried for tea. To dry the leaves, we bundle them and hang them upside down by their stems.

"Comfrey remains one of my favorite herbs despite the controversy surrounding it. I've found it works wonders in healing wounds, as a poultice for sprained ankles and torn ligaments, and as a tea for broken bones."

— Rosemary Gladstar

RUSSIAN COMFREY *SYMPHYTUM X UPLANDICUM*

Plant Cycle: Perennial, Zones 3–9

Propagation: Comfrey is easily started from root cuttings, propagated by division, or grown from seed.

Parts Used: Leaf, root

Rosemary

As you might expect, rosemary is one of Rosemary Gladstar's treasured green garden friends. The plant's strong fragrance lingers long after you've touched it, which is perhaps what has made rosemary a symbol for remembrance. Students in ancient Greece and Rome were known to wear rosemary behind their ears to help them remember their lessons. It is a favorite herb of crafters and is often used in making aromatic wreaths, potpourris, nosegays, soaps, and candles.

Traditional Medicinal Uses

Rosemary is a great antiseptic. Dried and powdered, it can be used as a dressing on wounds, and when infused in a tea, rosemary becomes a refreshing mouthwash that can also heal mouth ulcers and canker sores.

The essential oil of rosemary, when used in an aromatherapy diffuser, is excellent for refreshing a sickroom and enlivening the patient. It invigorates the nervous system without stressing it and can be used to relieve headaches. Rosemary essential oil has antifungal and antibacterial properties as well.

For respiratory problems, bathing with rosemary can break up congestion. To relieve cold-related nasal and chest congestion, add rosemary to a simmerpot and inhale the steam.

Rosemary also promotes healthy digestion and increases the production of bile. It especially aids in the digestion of fats, which may be the reason it is traditionally the seasoning of choice for fatty meats, such as pork and lamb. It is often a component of circulatory formulas because of its strengthening effects on the veins and arteries.

Growing and Harvesting

Rosemary is a Mediterranean plant. It likes to be watered, but it doesn't like wet feet. Allow it to dry out between waterings. It is the perfect candidate for raised beds or pots. And it loves full sun.

Choosing the Right Variety

There are many varieties of rosemary, each with its own peculiarities and needs. *Rosmarinus officinalis* can be trained into a standard, which becomes a hedge of swirling branches with tiny blue flowers. The standard 'Santa Barbara' and trailing rosemaries are great for low-growing ground covers. They look nice trailing down the sides of Grecian-type urns or out of cracks in walls. The 'Arp' cultivar is known as the most hardy and can survive below-freezing temperatures.

ROSEMARY AND ROSE BISCOTTI

½ cup butter	½ teaspoon salt
1 cup sugar	1 cup chopped almonds, toasted
3 eggs	
1 drop rose geranium oil	1 teaspoon finely chopped dried rosemary leaves
3 cups flour	
1 tablespoon baking powder	2 teaspoons finely chopped dried rose petals

Cream the butter and sugar. Add eggs one at a time, beating well. Add geranium oil. Sift flour, measure, and sift again with baking powder and salt. Add to the creamed mixture and stir in the almonds, rosemary, and rose. Knead until smooth, then cut the dough in half. Make two rolls about 2 inches in diameter. Bake at 350°F for 30 minutes, until firm. Slice, then toast on cookie sheets about 10 minutes.

ROSEMARY *ROSMARINUS OFFICINALIS*
Plant Cycle: Tender perennial,
Zones 8–11
Propagation: Rosemary is easily
started from stem cuttings or
layering.
Parts Used: Aerial parts

Bee Balm

Rosemary is a great fan of bee balm, and it's easy to see why. Bee balm was one of the first North American wildflowers to be brought into the garden by early settlers. It has whorls of glorious flowers 2 to 4 inches in diameter in many striking colors, from intense scarlet to soft pink and everything in between. These beautiful blooms attract hummingbirds and butterflies to dance about your garden. Remove spent flowers regularly for a continual bloom throughout the summer.

Traditional Medicinal Uses

Until recently, we grew only the red-flowering *Monarda didyma*, whose leaves we use to make a refreshing summer tea. Then Matthew Wood, an herbalist from Minnesota, came to visit the farm. He told wonderful stories of the healing uses of the purple-flowering *M. fistulosa*, also called wild bergamot. A Native American friend of Matthew's calls it sweet leaf, and you can definitely feel a soothing, sweet energy emanating from this plant.

We recommend reading Matthew's *Book of Herbal Wisdom* to learn more about Native American uses for monarda. Many tribes used monarda to treat everything from digestive disorders and menstrual difficulties to colds, flus, and headaches. In fact, *M. didyma* is also known as Oswego tea because of its importance as a healing herb to the Oswego tribe.

Growing and Harvesting

Although you can start monarda from seed, root divisions are easy to take and propagate well. Space the new divisions 12 inches apart.

After the first frost, cut the stems down to the ground and cover with mulch. In the second or third spring, dig up the root cluster and divide to give to friends or plant elsewhere in the garden. Otherwise your monarda will become an impenetrable thicket of tightly woven roots.

To harvest, simply snip off the aerial parts. The leaves, fresh or dried, make a refreshing summer tea.

"What would a garden be without bee balm, in all its many species, colors, and scents? I love the wild monarda the best . . . for its pungent, delicious odor, its bright purple flowers, and its usefulness. It is a wonderful herbal medicine and is considered a 'cure-all' by our native elders."

— Rosemary Gladstar

ELEGANT EDIBLE-FLOWER SALADS

Originally, salads were small bowls of bitter greens served before meals to aid digestion. During the creative expanse of Elizabethan times, salads became beautiful displays of greens, flowers, and herbs. Today, an edible-flower salad is the hit of any potluck. Some edible flowers you might use include:

- Monarda (pull the individual lipped flowers off the central head)
- Calendula (use the fresh petals only, not the whole flower)
- Rose petals (if they have been grown organically)
- Violets and pansies
- The petals of pinks
- Society garlic, chive, and garlic chive flowers
- Flowers of the crucifers, such as mustard, wild radish, and arugula
- Chopped lavender flowers

Bee Balm *MONARDA* SPP.
Plant Cycle: Perennial, Zones 3–9
Propagation: Bee balm is easily propagated by division.
Parts Used: Aerial parts

Deer Run Herb Sanctuary

one couple's retreat

Chenue and Barry Gill live in the beautiful rolling hills and oak country of the Napa Valley in California. Busy owners of a thriving health food store, they know the importance of "life after business hours." Barry, a retired professor, enjoys writing poetry and studying Eastern mysticism. Chenue, an artist and therapist, creates exotic jewelry and offers therapeutic insights in the realms of dream work. Their health food store sprang from their desire to help people live happier, healthier lives through good nutrition and herbs. Their gardens, which feature native plants and the plant medicines of Native Americans who inhabited their valley, are an homage to those who have walked their land before them.

◁ Barry often reads poetry to Chenue as she works in the garden. They consider the garden to be their personal peaceful retreat and have filled it with their favorite native plants.

Not every gardener aspires to be a public gardener. In fact, we suspect that most gardeners would prefer to maintain the anonymity of their gardens, seeking solitude in their own private space surrounded by green friends. Deer Run Herb Sanctuary is one such garden.

When they think of the golden state, most people from outside its boundaries immediately conjure up grand visions of Hollywood. But California has many faces: the mountains, the ocean, the farmlands of the great central valley, the desert. The famed vineyards of Napa Valley reside among the rolling hills of the coastal range. The area is famous for its wine, cuisine, hot springs, and gemstones. But it was the gentle, natural beauty of the region that brought Chenue and Barry to the Napa foothills.

Their land is sometimes influenced by the Pacific Ocean — cool, moist, and occasionally foggy. At other times the climatic influence comes from the central valley — intensely hot and dry. Friends laughed when Chenue and Barry first found the house and land that eventually became Deer Run Herb Sanctuary. They told them, "The house is a wreck, the land too arid, and the location too far out." Ten years and lots of work later, however, Deer Run Herb Sanctuary is a gathering place of beauty, comfort, and peace for their friends and family.

▷ Set in the rolling, golden hills of northern California, Deer Run Herb Sanctuary is a place of reflection and tranquillity.

When Chenue and Barry first moved onto the property, their vision was that of an English country garden. One of Chenue's favorite books as a child was *The Secret Garden,* by Frances Hodgson Burnett, and she had in mind something akin to the charming and timeless garden in that story. She wanted her garden to be a sanctuary where she could go at the end of the day and let her worries melt away. Her dream garden was beautiful and fragrant, yet practical. She envisioned a garden that would provide culinary herbs, edible flowers, and some of the basic medicinal herbs, as well as bright and cheery flowers to bring color and fragrance into the house.

Chenue and Barry both wanted the garden to be an outdoor extension of their living space. They wanted not a garden that would be viewed from inside the house and admired through the windows, but a garden that was a welcoming space wherein they could entertain guests and spend time relaxing and sharing with each other.

They spent the first year tilling the garden and laying out the pathways. Then Chenue and Barry set to planting their English garden. They favored the English style of being somewhat casual, slightly more free form than other, more formal gardens.

However, vision is one thing and application is another. Most of the plants set out that year failed. The delicate medicinals and English garden flowers were just too fragile for the severe weather and vagaries of this site.

Upon the failure of their first garden efforts, Chenue and Barry decided to inventory the plant life already growing on their eight-acre parcel. They were quickly astounded by the variety of plant life they found. The land is a combination of chaparral and oak forest. Some of the plants growing wild there are California bay, cleavers, miner's grass, blackberry, bracken, buckthorn, buckeye, ferns, chickweed, iris, penstemon, manzanita, milk thistle, several varieties of oak, mistletoe, wild oats, clover, sheep sorrel, and usnea. In spring the ground is dotted with a wonderful variety of colorful wildflowers.

The project of cataloging the botanicals on this property taught Chenue and Barry a valuable lesson. They learned that their seemingly dry and barren landscape was actually a treasure trove of plant diversity. They began to see the value of preserving the wildness of the land and realized that their garden could be used to enhance and supplement this wildness, rather than to domesticate and civilize this land.

◁ Beginning gardeners need not fear that gardens filled with herbs will be a monochromatic green. Herbs have many hues and forms to offer. Here the silver and blue of Russian sage and the violet-pink of echinacea add festive color to the garden landscape.

CATALOGING YOUR WEEDS

"What is a weed?

A plant whose virtues

have not yet

been discovered."

— *Ralph Waldo Emerson*

If you move into an undeveloped area or have decided to preserve a part of your land as untamed, it is well worth the effort to catalog your wild plants. Cataloging is a great way to become intimate with your land. Which weeds grow where will tell you much about your soil and water tables. Through your research you will most likely get to know the history of your area as well, and perhaps even the traditional uses of the plants on hand. Whether you decide to keep a written record or create an album of pressed specimens, you will be creating a legacy for those who follow.

To start, simply walk slowly over your land. Note what grows where and its stage of growth. Purchase reliable field guides specific to your area. You will most likely need to buy more than one, as no one guide has every plant. If you are having trouble finding guides, college bookstores often have a good selection. Also check with the staff of your Parks and Recreation Department to see whether they offer wild plant identification walks.

How you record your findings is up to you. Some people write directly into the guidebooks, noting the place and date of the discovery of a particular plant. Others keep journals in book form or on a computer database. Those more artistically inclined may keep sketchbooks or pressed plant books and include their notes. If you have children, a book created by the family together is a wonderful keepsake.

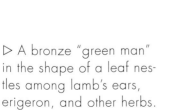
▷ A bronze "green man" in the shape of a leaf nestles among lamb's ears, erigeron, and other herbs.

Since the lesson of that first garden failure, Chenue and Barry have concentrated on growing plants that either currently reside or may have resided on this property naturally. They focus on plants that require little maintenance. They use strictly organic methods and water and feed the garden sparingly — these are plants accustomed to thriving without pampering.

The garden is now predominantly a California native-plant garden, with a few hardy exotics and garden flowers mixed in to satisfy Chenue and Barry's original vision of an English country garden. Although some of the plants are not native, all of them are drought tolerant, a must in an area where it is not uncommon for the well to run dry.

Chenue often travels around the San Francisco Bay Area looking for native-plant sales, usually with a list in hand and a familiar promise to Barry — not to come home with a trunkful of new plants — still ringing in her ears. The list comes in handy, but the promise is rarely kept. She must weigh her plant purchases carefully, though, because she and Barry are working with a limited supply of water. Before buying any plant, Chenue must consider whether she has enough water to support the new acquisition without risking the water supply for the rest of the garden's inhabitants.

Careful selection has given Chenue and Barry the luxury of being able to spend much of their time enjoying the garden, rather than maintaining it. They feel a sense of satisfaction in doing their part to preserve a variety of native plants, and their garden rewards them by affording them the free time to just "be" there.

△ A blue gazing ball gives a central focus to this abundant screen of echinacea, salvia, and Russian sage.

△ ▷ Chenue and Barry have a great respect for the history of herbal medicine. Chenue collects antique medicine bottles, which offer useful clues to healing potions of the past and a connection to the legacy of traditional herbal medicine. The health food store Chenue and Barry own and manage is a modern-day village apothecary. Here Barry weighs out herbs for customers in much the same manner as that of pharmacists of centuries ago.

These Napa gardeners feel a strong connection to the earth. They try to live their lives so as to be a part of their habitat. Chenue and Barry have spent countless hours observing the ways of the natural inhabitants that share the land with them. They tell us that they have learned some of their most valuable life lessons from the plants themselves.

Chenue admires the wildflowers in particular for their ability to survive difficult conditions. They are to her an important symbol of death and resurrection, and her gardens are always a haven for these beautiful ambassadors of the "weed" world. Those who are fortunate enough to meet Chenue will immediately see the connection. Like the wildflower, Chenue is a "wild woman": persevering and strong, yet beautiful and seemingly delicate.

Chenue and Barry are still working on creating a database of lost or little-known medicinal and food uses of the local native plants. They feel that part of living in concert with nature is knowing the full extent of what nature can provide and how to use it.

Soon after Chenue and Barry began their native-plant garden, they partnered up and took over a natural foods store. As she began to acquaint herself with the herbs for sale in her shop, Chenue was overjoyed to find that she was rediscovering many old and dear companions that she had previously known just as garden plants. She was to learn that not only were the herbs in her garden beautiful, but they had many historical uses as well.

To increase their herbal knowledge, Chenue and Barry attended the California School of Herbal Studies, when Rosemary Gladstar was the director. Chenue was inspired, as are so many others, under the tutelage of Rosemary. She brought her new understanding of herbs and their possibilities back to Napa Valley, where she put them to good use in the store and at home.

It was at the California School of Herbal Studies that we first crossed paths with Chenue and Barry, as Shatoiya was then studying with Rosemary as well. We found them to be a delightful couple filled with inspiration, fun, and love. We have been close friends ever since.

◁ Violas, salvias, and other edible flowers can enhance both the flavor and the presentation of garden salads and other dishes.

Chenue and Barry's Favorite Herbs

Chenue and Barry are great believers in growing native plants, and their favorite herbs — madrone, sage, and mugwort — reflect that devotion.

Madrone

A madrone tree shedding its wine-colored bark

Madrone is beloved by all who encounter it, including Chenue and Barry. This graceful tree's natural range is from the southern California coast up through British Columbia. The tree sports a sleek, reddish brown trunk; shiny, dark green leaves about 5 inches long; and beautiful, bell-shaped, pinkish white spring flowers that hang in clusters from the branches.

In fall the plant is decorated with red berries, a favorite food for local birds. Madrone is constantly shedding — bark, leaves, and berries — so it may be considered messy in a formal garden. In a wild, natural setting, this constant cycle of exfoliation makes it quite exquisite.

Traditional Medicinal Uses

Native Americans living in what is now California made a tea to treat colds from madrone bark, roots, and leaves and a wash to cleanse wounds from the leaves and bark. They also harvested the berries to eat raw, cooked, dried, or fermented and made into cider. To the modern palate, the berries can be pithy and not very tasty; wild-plant gourmands will probably want to add some sugar or honey to foods made with the berries. The leaves are sometimes used like uva-ursi for bladder, yeast, and vaginal infections.

Madrone flower essence is warm and comforting. It's a wonderful emotional balm for anyone going through a nerve-wracking transitional period

Growing and Harvesting

Madrone does best in a loamy acidic soil and full sun. It thrives away from areas where cold air gathers and when sheltered from the wind. To grow this tree, you need to mimic some of its native conditions: quick-draining, dry soil and a sunny exposure. Once established, a madrone tree should be watered deeply but infrequently.

"My favorite thing on our property is the madrone tree. In early spring it starts with a dull brown bark just like all the other trees. You'd never guess the magical surprises it holds in store. The brown starts to peel and reveals this smooth and beautiful red-wine color. As if that weren't enough, the red soon cracks away to reveal the final secret, the shocking chartreuse green underneath. I love these madrone colors so much, I used them to paint the bathroom."

— *Chenue Gill*

MADRONE *ARBUTUS MENZIESII*
Plant Cycle: Tree, Zones 7–9
Propagation: Unless you
have a super-green thumb,
buy a young tree from a
reputable nursery.
Parts Used: Leaves, berries

Sage

There are so many types of sage, and so many reasons to love each one. There are decorative salvias, like *Salvia farinacea* Victoria Hybrids or 'Blue Bedder', pineapple sage *(S. elegans)*, and Mexican bush sage *(S. leucantha)*. Clary sage *(S. sclarea)*, much beloved by hummingbirds, has beautiful broad leaves and sends up small but showy white and purple flowers. California coastal white sage *(S. apiana)* is revered as a smudging herb and is often burned in spiritual rituals for clarity and cleansing. Garden sage *(S. officinalis)* is probably the best-known sage and is used both for medicine and in cooking.

Traditional Medicinal Uses

The tea of *S. officinalis* is a good all-around preventive for when you feel *something* coming on but you're not sure what that something is. Teas made with sage help fend off colds and flus and also make a great gargle for relieving and healing sore throats. Sage is antiseptic in nature and is often used as an ingredient in salves for rashes and cuts.

Caution: Sage should not be used during pregnancy and is not for nursing mothers — it will dry up breast milk.

Sage in the Kitchen

There's an old saying that goes something like "Ladies who would live for aye [forever] must eat sage in May." It's referring to sage's reputation as an herb of immortality and wisdom. To comply with this "sage" advice, we make delicious fritters by dipping the leaves of garden sage in a tempura batter, frying them in a bit of vegetable oil, and serving them with soy sauce.

"I love the fragrance of salvias. When you brush against them, they seem to be speaking to you with their smell. . . . I love to bundle them into smudge sticks and give blessings with them."

— *Chenue Gill*

MAKING A SMUDGE STICK

To make a smudge stick: Lay out on a table half of a single sheet of newspaper. Cut the herbs of your choice the same length as the shorter length of the paper. Our favorite herbs are rosemary, lavender, sage, and artemisia. Keep the herbs on their stems.

Gather as much as will comfortably fit into the circle made by your thumb and first finger. Lay the bundle at the bottom edge of the paper. Tightly roll up the herbs in the paper, like a big cigar, and put a rubber band on each end. Put in a warm place to dry. In about two weeks, unroll the bundle and remove the paper. The herbs should stay in shape on their own. Wrap your smudge stick in colorful yarn or cotton crochet string. Store in a basket in a cool, dry location.

To use a smudge stick: Carefully light the end of the stick with a match. Wait a moment, as you do when lighting a stick of incense, and then extinguish the flame and blow on the glowing end to encourage your smudge stick to smoke. Hold a plate underneath it to catch ashes.

Fan the stick back and forth so that the smoke drifts over the area that needs a change of energy: yourself, the room, an object. When you are finished smudging, put out the smoldering stick by tamping it in a pot of sand or dirt.

Smudge sticks

SAGE *SALVIA* SPP.

Plant Cycle: Perennial, biennial, or annual depending on species

Propagation: Salvias are easy to start from seed or cuttings.

Parts Used: Leaves

Mugwort

Chenue and Barry tell us that mugwort is one of their favorite herbs. Once a favorite ingredient of beer makers, mugwort was the wort (herb) of the mug (tankard). In herbal circles mugwort is considered a magical and mystical herb. Said to increase psychic perception, it is often burned as a sacred herb and is an ingredient in many talismans and magic potions. Its reputation for inducing dreams is well earned, and it is often mixed with relaxing herbs in dream pillows. These pillows are helpful for those doing dream-work therapy or those who just love having an active night life!

Traditional Medicinal Uses

Mugwort is a bitter; hence, it is an aid to digestion. Bitter herbs help "wake up" the whole digestive system, allowing better absorption of nutrients. Mugwort is also used to treat menstrual disorders and, being of the *Artemisia* genus, is an effective vermifuge.

Externally, a wash of mugwort steeped in vinegar is excellent for poison oak and ivy. Chinese healers have used mugwort for centuries in the form of *moxa*. Moxa is similar to incense in its cone or stick form and is burned over or on the skin at specific acupuncture points to release dammed-up energy. When these energy points are released, it increases circulation to the meridians to help heal any number of conditions.

In the Garden

The mugwort native to California, *Artemisia douglasiana*, is exceptionally fragrant. It grows straight and tall (3 to 6 feet), its long, narrow leaves showing deep green on one side and silver on the other. The common garden mugwort, *A. vulgaris*, grows lower and likes to ramble. Its leaves have the distinctive silver and green coloring but are smaller and less fragrant.

Both *A. douglasiana* and *A. vulgaris* can become invasive. Neither is too picky about soil or water. When our mugwort goes dormant in the winter, we cut back the leaves to the ground and mulch to protect the roots.

PLEASANT DREAMS TEA

1 part dried mugwort
1 part dried lavender flowers
1 part dried spearmint
½ part dried chamomile
½ part dried rose petals
¼ part dried rosemary

Blend ingredients together and store away from heat and light. To make a cup of tea, use 1 scant teaspoon of dried herbs per cup of water. Bring the water to a boil, pour over the herbs, cover, and let steep 10 minutes. Drink before bedtime for an exciting dream life.

Caution: This tea is not recommended for pregnant women or young children.

Mugwort *Artemisia vulgaris*
Plant Cycle: Perennial, Zones 4–8
Propagation: Mugwort is easy to propagate by division in late winter or early spring, or it can be started from seed.
Parts Used: Aerial parts

Plimoth Plantation

a living history

John Forti's life makes perfect sense if you believe in destiny. In his youth, John was surrounded by family and friends who gardened. And he grew up in Norwell, Massachusetts, an area steeped in Native American and early American culture and history. It was the ideal environment for cultivating a historical gardener.

In addition to tending plants at his home, a wooded cabin retreat, John is now the head horticulturalist at Plimoth Plantation, where he is responsible for the many recreated Pilgrim gardens and several teaching and historic gardens contained within Plimoth Plantation's 138-acre site. He has become an accomplished herbalist and an expert on the plants and medicines of seventeenth-century America.

◁ Visiting Plimoth Plantation offers more insight into the lives of Pilgrim settlers than does reading a library full of history books. Under the guidance and wisdom of horticulturalist John Forti, the gardens at Plimoth Plantation have become exact replicas of their Pilgrim ancestors.

Plimoth Plantation is a living-history museum that re-creates the village of the Plimoth Pilgrims of 1627, seven years after their landing at Plymouth Rock. It also offers a representational look into the lives of the Wampanoag Indians, who greeted the Pilgrims when they landed on the North American continent.

The houses of this twenty-first-century village were all constructed with the same materials and technology used by the early Pilgrims. They were a people well accustomed to living with what nature could provide and were consequently closely tied to the land. Much of the food was grown in fields outside the village walls, but each household had its own garden as well. These individual gardens supplemented their diets and served as a medicine chest for the family.

The caretakers and gardeners of this wonderful living-history center have done careful, painstaking research to discover just what plants you might have found in a Pilgrim's garden and to incorporate these plants into their gardens.

Staff members take on the persona of an individual who lived in the Pilgrim village at Plimoth. They are extremely well coached; talking with them helps visitors understand the earliest inroads of European culture into North America.

Strolling through the gardens is a great way to experience and connect with the day-to-day lives of the first European colonists. Seeing the similarities between the way the Pilgrims worked their gardens and what we do today helps us share our connection to all humans who survived by working the earth and sustained themselves with what the earth provided.

As visitors learn, the techniques of home gardening haven't changed all that much in hundreds of years. But there is one subtle difference. Many of us who garden nowadays do so mostly for the pleasure of it. After all, supermarkets across the continent carry fresh produce all year long. If our bean crop fails, we will survive. Gardening for most of us is an exercise in mental health, and the fact that we can produce foods and medicines from such a pleasurable activity is an added benefit.

For the Pilgrims, however, gardening was strictly a necessity. Though we're sure many of them enjoyed working in the warm sun and tilling the earth, the success or failure of their gardens had a direct impact on their survival. Their gardens were utilitarian — only plants with practical uses were allowed space in the garden.

Even before these early European settlers arrived, the land on which the living-history center is situated was farmed by the local indigenous population. For gardener John Forti, it is an honor to continue the work passed down from generation upon generation of earth stewards — from Native Americans to Pilgrims to farmers to the modern-day Plimoth Plantation — who have worked the land before him.

A traditional gathering basket filled with herbs and flowers

"Over the years, you get to know the herbs in your garden by their many different names and attributes. As with friends, your understanding and appreciation of the herbs grows richer with the accumulated knowledge of the years."

— John Forti

◁ One of the Plimoth Plantation staff members in her Pilgrim persona harvests lavender, ladies' bedstraw, and yarrow using the same tools and techniques that her seventeenth-century counterpart would have been accustomed to.

We've visited Plimoth Plantation a number of times, and it's been our good fortune to get to know John Forti. John finds his inspiration in the works of herbalists and gardeners of the seventeenth century, and he has spent countless hours reading cookbooks, herbals, and gardening literature from that era. Through his research, John is getting to know the people who lived in Plymouth during the seventeenth century. By understanding what they perceived to be true, he has gained insights into their thought processes. Whether their information on nutrition or medicine is accurate based on what we know today is not of important to John in his role as a

historical horticulturist. What is important is to see the world as the early Pilgrims saw it.

There is an old saying that history was written by the winners. Much has been published about grand campaigns, wars, and great social movements. That's interesting stuff, but many of us also wonder how the common man and woman lived throughout our history.

There is now a movement among historians to study "microhistory" — the story of the individual lives of common people. Have you ever wondered what it was like to live as a Pilgrim during the first years of their colony? People like John Forti help communicate that to us. Knowing the history of war and political change tells us how humans from another place came to live in a continent called North America, but it's knowing how common individuals acted and thought in their daily lives that tells us how humanity and culture survived and became what they are today.

◁ As part of his work at Plimoth Plantation, John occasionally portrays the Pilgrim surgeon Samuel Fuller. He also conducts herb walks and garden tours, sans colonial garb, for visitors.

▷ The plant selection in the Fuller garden at Plimoth Plantation is based on *The Admirable Secrets of Physic and Chyrurgery*, a 1699 compilation of the writings of the early surgeons of the Plymouth colony, of which Samuel Fuller was the first.

△ A costumed staff member collects borage flowers. In the seventeenth century, these cucumber-flavored edible flowers were often added to salads. They were thought to be good for the blood and to bring courage.

When John Forti took over the gardens of Plimoth Plantation, his first duty was to continue the research begun by his predecessors. He began making minor changes in the gardens to reflect more accurately the subsistence-level horticulture the Pilgrims practiced. It was important not only to have the proper plants in the garden but also to show them in the proper proportions. He wanted to be sure that each garden was an accurate reflection of what a Pilgrim family might have grown in 1627.

This work even included removing perennial plants of a maturity greater than that of the Pilgrim colony's. For example, a fifteen-year-old domestic rosebush could not have existed in a Pilgrim garden in 1627 because the settlers had been on the American continent only seven years. John arranged to have those plants dug up and replaced them with new, younger plants.

Throughout history gardeners have saved seeds from their gardens, selecting seeds from those plants with the most desirable characteristics. These "heirloom" seeds retained the genetic diversity needed to maintain a viable garden.

Modern agriculture has taken to using hybrid seeds produced by scientifically crossing strains to create plants with desired characteristics, such as uniform growth patterns and simultaneous maturation for ease of harvesting. This genetic "cloning" can benefit the commercial grower. However, the danger of forfeiting biodiversity to enhance production is that genetically standardized crops can be wiped out en masse by blight or disease.

Seeds from hybrid crops cannot be saved, because succeeding generations deteriorate into an inferior image of the original parent plant. This makes farmers dependent on seed companies, and hence less self-sufficient. Heirloom seeds, on the other hand, produce plants that are hardy and genetically diverse, and they preserve the genetic legacy that is a part of our history.

As a museum, Plimoth Plantation strives to maintain living collections of historically significant plants and animals. By making these heritage plants available to the public, Plimoth Plantation promotes preservation and genetic diversity among today's gardeners.

Pictured on pages 88–89: Designed by John Forti, this garden models the plant selections and gardening techniques that would have been used by the Pilgrim family living in this home.

"Herbal lore is often either taken as gospel or used to belittle the concept of herbalism. I feel that accurate research is paramount to the herbal renaissance taking place today."

— John Forti

"My grandparents would speak of eating the fruits of your own labors and how it was better to pay the grocer than the doctor. I still believe these things to be true, but over the years, as I prepare medicine and food from the things I grow, I find equal comfort in gardening and all of its outgrowth as a meditative and spiritual practice."

— *John Forti*

For a nonprofit educational institution with a mission larger than horticulture alone, staffing is always something of a struggle. John must use all his ingenuity and resourcefulness to create and maintain his gardens. Like most proud gardeners, he cringes when his gardens are not up to par. However, the Pilgrims' records lend some comfort, as they speak of kitchen gardens "oft being deformed by the seasons."

John must deal with many of the same challenges his Pilgrim predecessors had, and — as caretaker of a public garden — a few they would never have imagined. The high level of foot traffic, erosion, and general wear and tear takes its toll on the gardens. On the other hand, the Pilgrims' occasionally tumultuous relationship with their Native American neighbors is an issue that John is thankful the museum handles better today.

△▷ Sturdy raised beds containing fertile, well-composted soil allowed the early Pilgrims to grow bountiful supplies of vegetables and herbs, including onions, cabbage, beets, orach, and borage.

Feverfew

"The entire process of gardening is as much a therapy for me as the herbalism and healthy diet that are its end result. The good fortune in gardening is that it also provides me the flowers to share with others."

— *John Forti*

Like all gardeners, the Pilgrims were deeply invested in the health and condition of their garden soil. Most of the Pilgrim household gardens were in raised beds from 1 to 3 feet deep and built narrow enough for a person to be able to reach to the middle of the garden from the alleyways on either side. The length of the gardens was determined by the family's requirements for an adequate harvest. The sides were built up with wood, rock, or bricks, and, of course, replenishing the soil with compost and manure was a continual process.

Gardeners of early North America, both natives and immigrants, planted and harvested by the phases of the moon. They planted root crops with the new moon, and they planted crops that grew above the ground so that they would sprout with the full moon. Herbalists gathered their herbs during the full moon, believing that, like the ocean tides and women's courses, the juices and oils that are often the plant's strength will also be on the rise.

John's study of seventeenth-century gardening techniques has taught him some lessons he'd like to pass on:

• If you are gathering a plant for its medicinal or nutritional properties, observe where the plant is currently investing its energy. By doing so you will know how to gather the plant's vital energy. Look to harvest the flowers and tops of the plants in the spring and early growing season; gather the roots during the fall, after the first frost.

• One seventeenth-century saying goes, "A cook is half a physician." This sentiment reflects a belief that if you incorporate a wide variety of herbs and seasonal produce into your diet, your food becomes your primary medicine. Many cultures around the world practice the concept of seasonal diets, understanding that the body has different requirements during the different seasons.

GARDEN WISDOM FROM THE WAMPANOAG INDIANS

Most of us remember from elementary school the story of Native Americans teaching the Pilgrims gardening techniques suitable for the climate they had moved to, including using dead fish as a fertilizer. The secret of Wampanoag planting is a system that enriches the soil, requires less labor than traditional gardening, and still produces a wonderful harvest.

Start by digging a 6-inch-deep hole and putting a dead fish in it. You may use fish emulsion, but you'll get better results with a whole fish. Cover the fish and create a mound about 5 inches tall. Space these mounds about 3 feet apart. In the center of the mound, plant four or five corn seeds. When the corn is 3 to 5 inches tall, plant pole beans around the corn-stalks and squash around the base of the mound.

You have now created a self-contained, self-supporting system. The corn will serve as stakes for the beans. The squash will shade the soil and discourage animals from stealing your harvest. The corn will take nitrogen from the soil, and the beans will return the nitrogen to the soil.

John Forti says, "I look forward to being a craggy old gardener." He sees gardening as a personal learning experience. He thinks of plants as story-tellers, because they remind him of the friends who passed along the seeds or root cuttings. He remembers the names by which his friends knew these plants and how they taught him to use them.

Each spring, when the gardens come to life again, he recalls the places he traveled to, how the different plants came to him, and the inspiration they provided. He considers his work in the gardens of Plimoth Plantation to be a unique opportunity to preserve the plants and teach an understanding of herbalism from the past to the present to the future.

▽ The Humoural Garden is a modern exhibit that John designed to teach visitors about the theory of medicine prevalent at the time of the Pilgrims. The Doctrine of Humours holds that illness is caused by the imbalance of melancholic, choleric, sanguine, and phlegmatic elements of the body. This system of understanding herbs and food is akin to Chinese and Ayurvedic medicine but works with plants familiar to practitioners of Western herbalism.

A Pilgrim's Garden
at Plimoth Plantation

GARDEN FEATURES

Bed A contains speedwell, lavender, St.-John's-wort, rue, bedstraw, comfrey, southernwood, horehound, yarrow, white lily, celandine, carduus benedictus, and marjoram.

Bed B contains hyssop, pennyroyal, tansy, elecampane, clary sage, angelica, winter savory, sage, rosemary, and thyme.

Bed C contains endive, coriander, chicory, and green beets

Bed D contains parsley, calendula, rocket, and lovage.

Bed E contains roses, gillyflower, and borage.

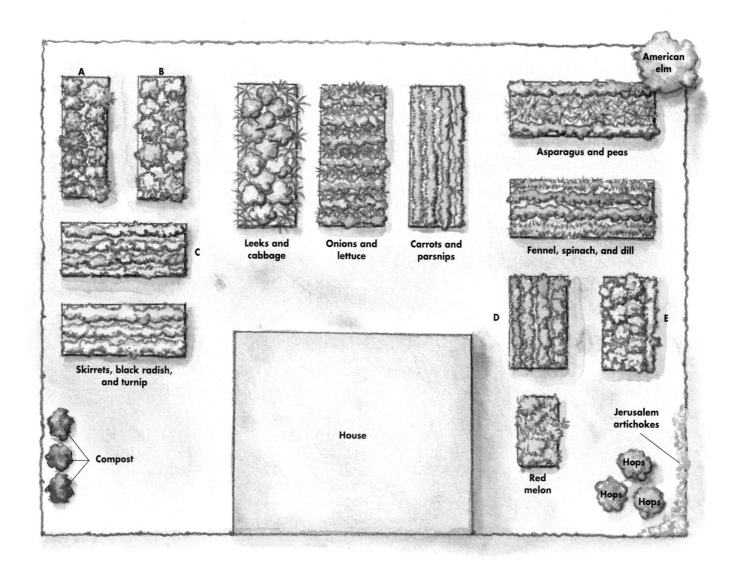

◁ Historic roses and avens demonstrate how beauty grows freely in what John terms "humble, subsistence-level gardens of the common people in the early years of the Plymouth colony."

◁ Even the animals at Plimoth Plantation are true representations of their Pilgrim ancestors. These Arapawa goats, for example, are a heritage breed from Arapawa Island in New Zealand. They are among the few surviving descendants of the native English milch (milk) goat, which is now extinct.

John's Favorite Herbs

When we asked John what his favorite herbs are, he listed three classic plant medicines of the Pilgrims: elecampane, yarrow, and calendula.

Elecampane

Elecampane has a long and venerable history; the ancient Romans used it to treat indigestion, and Pliny recommended it for lifting the spirits. Today, elecampane is widely recognized as a substitute for at-risk herbs like osha and lomatium.

Traditional Medicinal Uses

Elecampane has a strong affinity with the respiratory system. It is used for all types of lung complaints, including bronchitis, asthma, and even tuberculosis. The volatile oils stimulate expectorant action and the mucilage has a soothing, relaxing effect on the mucous membranes.

Elecampane is also a strong antiseptic and antimicrobial. In the past it was used as a wash to disinfect wounds.

WET, COLD COUGH TEA

1 part dried elecampane root
½ part dried echinacea root
½ part dried licorice root
½ part dried fennel seeds
½ part dried wild cherry bark
¼ part dried angelica root
¼ part dried marsh mallow root

Combine the herbs. Measure 1 teaspoon of herbs per cup of water. Add the herbs to the cold water, cover, and bring to a boil. Reduce the heat and simmer for 15 minutes, then strain. Drink as needed to help relieve heavy, phlegmy coughs.
Caution: Pregnant women should not take this tea.

Like angelica (see page 38), elecampane's bitter principle aids digestion. It is said that Julius Augustus ate elecampane roots every day to help his digestion and to "cause mirth."

The powerful flavor of elecampane's acrid resin and bitter principle can be unpleasant for someone tasting it for the first time. Because of this, elecampane is used medicinally but is not generally thought of as an herb for everyday tea.

Growing and Harvesting

Elecampane is a strikingly beautiful plant. It can reach 5 to 8 feet in height and has long, oval-shaped leaves that are sage green on the top and fuzzy white underneath. Beautiful composite flowers in multiple shades of gold adorn the tops of its green branches.

Elecampane is most happy when growing in full sun or dappled shade. It is adaptable to many soils but prefers fertile, moist, yet well-draining conditions. Give each plant at least a 3-foot-diameter plot in which to grow.

The roots are most potent when harvested in their second or third year. Digging them up takes a sharp shovel and a strong back. A large crown covered with buds stands at the soil's surface, while thick, tenacious roots spread from it deep into the ground.

We dig around the whole lot, the best we can, to pull up crown and roots. Then we use a pruning saw to cut off the roots, which we slice and dry for medicinal purposes. We also saw apart the crown buds and put them back in the ground so that they'll sprout and grow again.

ELECAMPANE *INULA HELENIUM*
Plant Cycle: Perennial, Zones 4–9
Propagation: Start elecampane
from seed or from divisions in fall
or spring when plant is dormant.
Part Used: Root

Yarrow

Yarrow is another of John's favorite herbs, and we can see why. A common thread in the teachings of various Native American tribes is that if a plant grows in abundance, it is meant to be used abundantly. We have been firsthand witnesses to yarrow's tenacious tendencies. One October morning we got up at 3:30 to hike a favorite trail by the light of the full moon. When we reached the top of the 10,000-foot-high peak, it was extremely cold and the wind was howling. We witnessed a beautiful sunrise, and as it illuminated our surroundings, we scanned the craggy shale for signs of life. We were amused and delighted to find only a solitary yarrow plant, growing where nothing else could in that hostile environment.

Traditional Medicinal Uses

Yarrow has a centuries-old reputation for healing. Its genus name, *Achillea*, comes from its use by the warrior Achilles to heal the wounds of his troops. It has hemostatic properties, meaning that it stops bleeding, and we have used it successfully for both nosebleeds and deep wounds. Its antiseptic constituents keep wounds from becoming infected, while its astringent properties speed their healing.

These same antiseptic and astringent constituents make yarrow a perfect ingredient for cosmetics and facial splashes and steams. Yarrow is also an effective ingredient in foot baths for athlete's foot, especially when combined with calendula (see page 101), which has antifungal properties.

Yarrow also has an affinity with the urinary system and is used to encourage the healing of bladder and other urinary tract infections. As an astringent, it's helpful in addressing bed-wetting and incontinence.

Yarrow is also antipyretic. As a tea or in a lukewarm bath, it helps balance fevers, allowing them to do their work but not to get so hot that they cause injury. Because of this fever-regulating potential, yarrow is exellent in flu formulas.

Growing and Harvesting

Yarrow is a great herb for beginners because it is easy to grow, has many medicinal uses, and is beautiful in flower. It loves full sun and acid soil but is adaptable to lots of places and conditions. Yarrow flowers form an umbrella of tiny, daisylike blossoms on top of a long stem that rises above fernlike leaves. Although the white-flowering yarrow (*Achillea millefolium*) is the species used medicinally, other yarrows come in a fantastic range of colors, including salmon, deep scarlet, bright gold and yellow, lavender, and pink. It generally blossoms from early summer to fall.

For a continual bloom, deadhead fading blossoms at the next leaf joint. For medicinal use, harvest the flowering stalks while they're in bloom, about a third of the way down a stem, just above a leaf joint. The stems will continue to grow and bloom all summer long.

To dry, tie small bundles of harvested yarrow at the bottom of the stems and hang upside down. When dry, strip the leaves and flowers from the stems and store for later use.

After the first frost, cut all the flower stems to the ground. Toss the harvested plant material into your compost pile.

"I look upon yarrow much as I do mint. It is not easily confined in the garden, but it is simple in its beauty, and as an herbalist, I find it is one of the most useful medicinal plants I grow."

— John Forti

Yarrow *ACHILLEA MILLEFOLIUM*
Plant Cycle: Perennial, Zones 3–9
Propagation: Yarrow is easily
started from seed or root division.
Parts Used: Flowering aerial parts

Calendula

Calendula was a favorite herb of the Pilgrims. It has become one of John's favorites as well, and we love calendula too. We have spots of the vibrant orange and yellow flowers in every corner of our garden, although we intentionally planted them in only one place. Their cycle from seed to blossom to seed again can be quite rapid, especially if you don't keep up the deadheading. Birds love to carry the seeds and plant them all over the garden.

Calendula is the perfect plant teacher for young gardeners. The moon-shaped seeds are easy to handle and germinate in just seven to ten days, so they can see results quickly. And what results! The masses of beautiful bright flowers are sure to delight gardeners of all ages.

Traditional Medicinal Uses

Calendula flowers have an affinity with the skin. They are often mixed with other skin-nurturing herbs, such as lavender and red clover, to make a delicious tea to enhance the skin, or are made into a salve for external use. Calendula is also antifungal and can be used as a mouth rinse for thrush in babies or adults. It is often recommended for candida and yeast infections.

Calendula is an aid for a wide range of digestive problems; it is often combined with chamomile and comfrey as a soothing tea for stomach upsets. Its antiviral and lymph-cleansing properties make it helpful in a tea during flu season.

Growing and Harvesting

Calendula seedlings are susceptible to a fungus called damping-off. However, watering them with a room-temperature tea of chamomile or nettle will prevent this fungus from developing. Mature plants sometimes develop powdery mildew. When this happens, we usually just cut the plants back to young healthy growth, and they come back strong and vigorous.

Most herbs should be harvested first thing in the morning, after the dew has dried but before the sun is high. However, bright yellow calendula is a plant of the sun. When picking the flowers for medicine, harvest during the hottest portion of the day, when the healing resins will have risen to the surface of the flower. We pick calendulas on the stem, just above a leaf joint. Then we cut the flower from the stem, close to the sepal, and spread the golden blossoms on a screen to dry.

In cooking, use only the petals. Fresh petals brighten green salads or can be added to cake and scone recipes. Calendula is also called poor man's saffron, and it lends a warm, delicate flavor and color to rice.

"Calendula speaks clearly to the overlap between food, medicine, cosmetic, and aesthetic that was so common in the seventeenth century."

— John Forti

DRY CREEK HERB FARM'S CLEAR SKIN TEA

1 part dried calendula flowers
1 part dried nettle leaves
1 part dried lavender tops
1 part dried red clover blossoms
1 part dried comfrey leaves

Blend herbs. Using 1 teaspoon of herbs per cup of water, bring the water to a boil. Pour over the herbs, cover, and let steep 15 minutes. Drink 2 to 4 cups daily as needed. This tea can also be used as a wash or added to a bath. This same herb combination is excellent in a soap or salve.

CALENDULA *CALENDULA OFFICINALIS*

Plant Cycle: Annual

Propagation:
Calendula grows easily from seed sown directly in the garden in spring.

Parts Used: Flowers

You don't just happen upon EverGreen Herb Garden — you really have to want to go there to actually get there. You find it at the end of a long, winding, narrow, bumpy road that clings to the sides of the steep canyons of the American River just north of Placerville, California. As in the classic story of Shangri-la, the harrowing trip is forgotten once you've come up the drive and are in the presence of the garden's magic.

EverGreen Herb Garden is, first and foremost, a meditation garden of serenity and beauty, a safe and comfortable space for students and visitors. It is also a learning center where Candis Cantin-Packard and Lonnie Packard teach a combination of Ayurvedic, Chinese, and Western herbalism.

The overall sense of EverGreen Herb Garden is one of tranquillity. This is a place to heal the soul, a place to slow down, wander the winding paths, listen to the faint ring of wind chimes, and inhale the occasional sweet fragrances of exotic flowers and herbs.

The meditative feel of the garden reflects the Eastern philosophies that Candis and Lonnie bring to their students. Because they integrate East Indian, Chinese, and Western herbalism, Candis and Lonnie have herbs from these regions growing in harmony, side by side.

As much as possible, Candis and Lonnie hold classes in the gardens. Candis feels that being among the plants helps students make connections with them, which is important for those learning a healing tradition centered on using plants as medicines. When it is hot, class is held in the shade of one of the stately oaks on the property or under an awning. An enclosed classroom for use in inclement weather is on the drawing board, but until it is finished, rainy-day classes are held in Candis and Lonnie's home.

Candis and Lonnie find their inspiration in our herbal elders. They admire Louis and Virginia Saso's ability to sustain their gardens and business for thirty years and respect Adelma Simmons of Caprilands not only for the longevity of her gardens but also for her ability to create so many small worlds within the gardens.

Candis's grandfather, Hercules Tsaklis, was perhaps her first gardening inspiration. She remembers that each year he planted and tended a beautiful vegetable garden. Although he has passed on, Candis is fortunate to still reap the rewards of her grandfather's labors; this past year she harvested some Bosc pears from a tree he planted more than sixty years ago. Candis says that eating fruit from a tree planted by her grand-father reminds her of the importance of the legacy we all leave behind. She hopes her children and her children's children will benefit from the gardens she and Lonnie have created.

"What is life

without a garden?"

— Candis Cantin-Packard

Pictured on pages 106–107:
A golden gazing ball reflects the burnished light of late afternoon, which illuminates the colorful columbine growing through-out the garden beds.

◁ Lush lawns invite visitors to take off their shoes and feel the green energy of the earth tickle the soles of their feet.

When Candis and Lonnie moved to the property now known as EverGreen Herb Garden, the house was painted brick red and had little or no discernible shade. Summer in the Sierra foothills can be intensely hot, so immediate changes had to be made to make the house cooler. After giving the house a new coat of a lighter-color paint, Lonnie and Candis planted wisteria, lilacs, and honeysuckle around the porches. Now visitors occasionally fail to notice the house beneath its shade-giving blanket of shrubs and flowers. In winter, the leaves fall from these plants, inviting the warming sun to come into the house through the windows.

With the house better prepared to endure the rigors of a northern California summer, Candis and Lonnie set out to create their gardens. Their land is set on a ridge top separating two forks of the American River. It is mostly flat, and scattered throughout the property are oaks and pines.

To protect their home and gardens from the threat of wildfire, Candis and Lonnie each year have cleared a portion of their property. In firefighting circles this is called creating a defensible perimeter. They cut back the brush with a saw or ax and pile the harvested branches in an open area. When the winter rains come, the brush piles can be burned safely. Candis and Lonnie started with the areas closest to the house and gardens and are slowly working their way out toward the edge of their property.

Like many gardeners, Candis and Lonnie are constantly dealing with the issue of water. The well on their property went dry shortly after they began gardening. They dug a second well, but this too went dry, just after a major expansion of the gardens. Fearing the loss of their gardens and the waste of all the labor used to put them in, Candis and Lonnie decided to dig their second well deeper.

Digging a well is never a sure thing, and Candis and Lonnie put all their hopes and prayers into the deepening of this well. Their prayers were answered at 700 feet. Just as they were considering declaring the well a failure, they hit an abundant and dependable source of water, and the well has produced consistently for them ever since. They added a 1,500-gallon holding tank as insurance.

Since that time Candis and Lonnie have purchased an adjacent three-acre parcel that has two wells on it. One of these wells is rated at 50 gallons per minute and has been set up with a solar well pump and a tank with the capacity to hold 2,500 gallons. Now they are confident that all their water needs in the foreseeable future will be met. Even when the power fails, they can provide for all their household and garden water needs.

Over the years Candis and Lonnie have become good friends of ours. We share stories and laugh about the similarities in our tales. Candis had already started work on her gardens when she met Lonnie; in him she found the perfect complement to her skills. Lonnie has an extensive background as a custom carpenter. He is an outstanding craftsman, and his high standards for the quality of his work are seen in every corner of the farm. They have the most beautiful woodshed and chicken coop we have ever seen. Lonnie is also a wonderful cook and regularly prepares meals for their guests and students.

When Candis first started the gardens, her vision was limited by what she alone could care for. When Lonnie came into her life, her dream grew. Two people with complementary skills can accomplish so much more than one person. When these two talented people joined their energy and dreams, the vision of EverGreen Herb Garden became manifest; it is now a self-sufficient learning center with lush, productive gardens and space for reflection and meditation.

▷ In the shade of a sweet gum tree, a water gnome, one of many "little spirits" that find their home at EverGreen Herb Garden, oversees a wild array of flowers.

Candis and Lonnie's EverGreen Herb Garden

GARDEN FEATURES

A Shade garden

B Ginseng and goldenseal bed

C Full-sun garden

D Culinary-herb garden

E Greenhouse

F Plant workstation

G Compost

H Chicken coop

I Willow tree

J Medicine-wheel garden

K Saint Francis garden

L Mandala garden

M Dry-loving plants

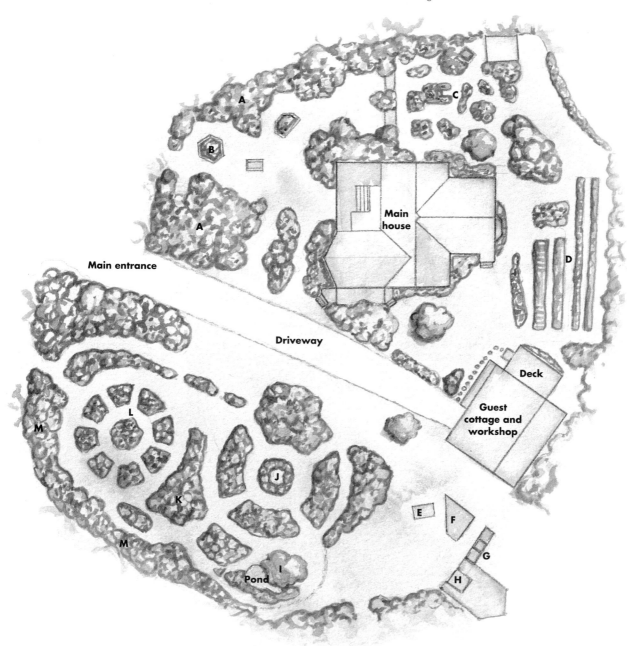

The medicine-wheel garden features lush lawns surrounded by herb and flower beds.

Saint Francis

At the entrance gate

Open pathways invite the visitor on long, leisurely strolls.

Water lilies

◁ Lonnie harvests the flowering tops of lavender.

△ A large bed of double-headed calendula creates a bright spot in the garden.

Like us, Candis and Lonnie

keep an assortment of interesting chickens. Among theirs is a pair of Egyptian chickens — wonderful layers and beautiful birds, sleek and colorful. However, they can be a bit aggressive; on one visit they wound up chasing our little dog in circles about the gardens! Candis and Lonnie also have a number of standard chickens and have found, as we have, that they are a great remedy for several garden pests.

Being a little farther out in the wilds than we are, Candis and Lonnie find that their chickens are more susceptible to predators. Lonnie built their chicken coop very sturdy and secure, and at night he and Candis make sure that all their chickens are all safely roosted in the coop before they retire themselves.

Each spring and fall EverGreen

Herb Garden is visited by a number of sandhill cranes. Those who live at the garden consider these visits to be blessed events, and all look forward to them with great anticipation. The first person to hear the cranes return will rush to tell the others.

The arrival of the cranes signals a change in the season. Their resonant call in spring signals rebirth; in fall, the time for harvest. Candis and Lonnie feel it is important to note these natural events. As you become attuned to living a more natural life, you will find that these events are more important to you than dates on the wall calendar.

"I do not live a day

without thinking of the

plants, seeing how

everyone is doing out

there, what new changes

have come about."

— Candis Cantin-Packard

EverGreen Herb Garden has hosted dozens of ceremonies and celebrations over the years, including baby blessings, memorials, and weddings. The gardens, the wildlife, and the profound quiet of this location all add a sense of timelessness and deep meaning to these special occasions.

After the loss of a dear friend to cancer, Candis and Lonnie held a memorial around their medicine wheel. Friends and family members all found this a touching and fitting way to remember their lost loved one. They buried his ashes in the soil in a corner of the wheel where he often spent time gardening. On this spot Candis and Lonnie have planted a hawthorn tree, which will serve as a living memorial.

For Candis and Lonnie, gardening is life. Their gardens provide for them and teach them. As Candis says, "My gardens speak to me about inner peace, about being in harmony with the seasons of our lives: birth, growth, death. They teach me how not to resist the changes of life, and about cooperation, expansion, acceptance, and the beauty of life."

Candis's son, Jonathan, enjoys a quiet moment in the garden.

▷ In spring, before the herbs and flowers have grown and spread, it's easy to see the geometric design of the medicine-wheel garden. Candis and Lonnie based the design of this garden on Louis and Virginia Saso's astrological garden (see pages 200–201).

Candis and Lonnie's Favorite Herbs

Candis and Lonnie's two favorite herbs, lavender and honeysuckle, have been the aromatic gems of the herb world for centuries. We too grow them in our garden.

Lavender

Lavender has been beloved by gardeners for centuries, so it was no surprise when Candis and Lonnie asked us to profile it as one of their favorite garden herbs. Lavender is used extensively in making herbal medicines and decorative crafts and is a staple in aromatherapy.

Traditional Medicinal Uses

Sweet-scented English lavender *(Lavandula angustifolia)* is the species most revered for its healing powers. It is a natural antidepressant; if you have the blues, place bowls of dried lavender all around your house and take lavender baths. A lavender bath before bedtime can also help promote a good night's sleep. An evening tea containing lavender may also be helpful (see Deep Sleep Tea, page 154).

Lavender's calming effect is wonderful for easing headaches. Just drink with other herbs in a tea, or rub a small amount of the essential oil on the temples and the back of the neck.

Lavender essential oil is one of the very few essential oils that can be used "neat," or undiluted, on the skin. The oil is a natural antiseptic and antimicrobial and was used in World Wars I and II to cleanse wounds. We once had a student at Dry Creek Herb Farm who was prone to keloids (heavy scarring) any time she cut herself. She noticed that if she applied lavender right away, she did not get scars.

A small amount of lavender essential oil added to distilled water in a mister makes an excellent spray for refreshing and gladdening a sickroom.

Growing and Harvesting

Plant lavender in full sun in dry, sandy soil. It dislikes having its feet wet. English lavender is quite hardy; when heavily mulched and planted in soil that drains well, it can survive a pretty harsh winter.

Harvesting lavender for medicinal purposes can be a tedious process. Ideally you want to harvest each stem, individually, when its buds are full to bursting but only one or two florets are open. Cut the stem below the flower, down to just above the next leaf joint. To dry, bundle six to nine stems together, secure with a rubber band, and hang upside down in a location away from direct sunlight and with good air circulation.

SHATOIYA'S SUNBURN OINTMENT

We have used this combination for healing and pain relief for sunburns, from mild burns to skin that has blistered. With more severe sunburns, we believe this blend has kept scars from occurring. It is also helpful for first-degree and shallow second-degree burns to help speed healing after initial first aid. If the burn covers a large area, try it on a small patch first to check for reactions.

1 part lavender essential oil
1 part St.-John's-wort infused oil
1 part aloe vera gel

Combine all ingredients in a small bottle. Shake well before use. Apply as needed. Store in a cool, dark location, where the ointment will keep for up to six months.

LAVENDER *LAVANDULA* SPP.
  Plant Cycle: Tender perennial
    to perennial, depending on
    species
  Propagation: Lavender can be
    started from seeds or cuttings.
  Parts Used: Aerial parts

Honeysuckle

A prolific climbing vine with fragrant flowers, honeysuckle is excellent for masking unsightly fences or crumbling garden walls. It can climb and cover just about anything in a very short period of time. A quite lovely part of our garden at Dry Creek Herb Farm is a privacy fence consisting of honeysuckle and star jasmine that separates us from our neighbors. When this "fence" is in bloom, the aroma is sublimely erotic. You'd never guess that underneath that abundance of green leaves and blossoms is a simple stretch of hog wire.

Our honeysuckle is a challenge, too, as it sends out many roots, and any part of the vine that touches the ground will start another plant. Our "fence" gets a severe cutting back twice a year, and even so we often find honeysuckle sneaking into other parts of the garden. If you're thinking of using a wall of honeysuckle as a screen, keep in mind that while most varieties are evergreen, some are deciduous, so whatever eyesore you're concealing may be visible for part of the year.

"I like blending the flowers of honeysuckle with petals from the flowers of one of my most fragrant rose bushes, 'Climbing Peace', to make a sun tea. The drink is so delightful."

— Candis Cantin-Packard

Traditional Medicinal Uses

Honeysuckle is most commonly used by practitioners of Chinese medicine; they call the flowers *jin yin hua*. The *yin* in the name gives us a clue that this is a cooling and sweet herb. The flowers are traditionally made into a tea that can be used to cool "hot" conditions such as infections, inflammations, and fever. Honeysuckle is also a common ingredient in Chinese formulas for detoxification; it has even been used to treat cases of food poisoning.

Externally, honeysuckle is effective as a wash for wounds and skin conditions such as poison oak, boils, and rashes. It can also be used for conjunctivitis.

Growing and Harvesting

Honeysuckle isn't picky about soil and will tolerate poor drainage. It can grow in full sun or partial shade. Once established, most varieties are fairly drought resistant. As there are many types, you should be able to find the variety that is most suitable for your area and purpose. Check in with your local gardening center for suggestions.

A TEA FOR FEVERISH FLU

Because it both stimulates immune function and reduces heat conditions, honeysuckle is an excellent herb for treating flus that are accompanied by fever.

2 parts dried lemon balm
1 part dried honeysuckle
1 part dried chrysanthemum flowers

1 part dried nettles
1 part dried wild oats tops

Combine all ingredients. Measure out 1 teaspoon of herbal blend per cup of water. Bring the water to a boil, pour over the dried herbs, and cover. Let steep 15 minutes, then strain. Sip frequently until all symptoms have passed.

HONEYSUCKLE *LONICERA JAPONICA*
Plant Cycle: Perennial,
Zones 4–11
Propagation: Honeysuckle is
easily started by layering.
Parts Used: Flowers

a little bit of country in the big city

Brian Fikes and Greg Howes share a home in the city of Sacramento. Though they have diverse talents and interests, they have in common a love of nature and the outdoors. Brian has a degree in behavioral sciences and a background in business, law, and accounting. However, he planted his first vegetable garden when he was just twelve, and he's kept his fingers well acquainted with the soil since then. Greg, on the other hand, has toured the United States and Europe as a professional ice skater and now puts his creative energy into the catering and restaurant field. Although he was born to true city slickers, he thoroughly loves gardening, and he enjoys being the caretaker of the flock of "designer" chickens that share the garden.

◁ Greg and Brian's charming garden is situated in the backyard of their city home, a green oasis that serves as a restful retreat from a fast-paced modern world.

Greg sharing a moment
with one of the chickens

"It is an undisputed fact

that the yard actually

belongs to the chickens.

We are merely the humble

caretakers."

— *Greg Howes*

This book is meant to inspire beginning gardeners and expose them to the physical, emotional, and spiritual benefits of gardening. One way we've tried to do that is by featuring the stories of some of North America's most well-loved herb gardens. But this is not the whole story of gardens in America. More common than the multi-acre public garden, of course, is the backyard garden, for with the urbanization of North America, many home gardeners today live in or very near a large metropolitan area.

With this in mind, we asked Brian Fikes and Greg Howes to allow us to tell the story of their beautiful garden, which is located in the backyard of their home in Sacramento, California.

We met Greg and Brian when they came to an herb workshop at our farm. We found them to be delightful company and enthusiastic students. They had been growing culinary herbs but now wanted to explore herbal medicine as well.

Both Greg and Brian enjoy the country and being surrounded by nature. At the present time, though, their careers keep them in the busy city of Sacramento. They hope someday to own a piece of land in a more rural setting where their vision of a country home with surrounding gardens and wild land can come to pass.

In the meantime, they bide their time in Sacramento. But living in the city does not mean you have to be surrounded by nothing but cement, steel, and glass. Greg and Brian decided that if they had to live in the city, they would at least make their little corner come alive with green things and the birds, insects, and small animals they would attract.

The main portion of their herb garden is only 12 feet by 6 feet. They supplement this main garden with a small container garden on the patio. The beauty of their garden is a testament to the fact that you don't need several acres to create a lovely and tranquil herb garden.

When Greg and Brian decided to create a country setting in their small city backyard, they began by driving around northern California to view public gardens. They visited all their gardening friends. They've drawn inspiration from every garden they've ever visited. Their belief is that all gardeners have their own way of expressing themselves in the dirt. Something can be learned from all of them, whether they are beginning gardeners or have been gardening since childhood.

Brian also drew inspiration from his family. His has many fond memories of his mother's garden. He remembers his excitement as a child at being able to eat foods the family had grown. For Brian, gardening offers a sense of security, something that calls to him from his first years.

Their garden started modestly. At first all the plants were in pots spread around the cement patio. They chose flowers that had a long blooming season and tended to blossom during late summer.

Then, because they greatly enjoy cooking, Greg and Brian decided to try growing a few culinary herbs, hoping to spice up their dishes. They found the herbs easy to grow, with delightful blooms, and they loved the idea of eating from their own garden. Now their garden is almost all herbs, with a little color thrown in for contrast.

"Green feels good. It has a calming effect on me. Tending the garden is like therapy."

— *Brian Fikes*

△ Sage is one of many herbs that thrive when grown in a container.

Greg and Brian face a unique challenge that none of the other gardeners in this book has to deal with: Their garden is on rental property. They are saving up to buy their own personal piece of green heaven, but for now they are forced to rent.

Many people enjoy the freedom that renting offers — when something in the house breaks, the landlord is responsible for fixing it. However, renting does limit what you can do with your garden. Digging a pond, for instance, is out of the question (although Brian and Greg hope to incorporate an aboveground water garden some day soon).

Working with any small space forces gardeners to reach a certain level of creativity. But renting ups the ante — you must be particularly inventive to grow a garden that is aesthetic, bountiful, and mostly portable. Because they rent, Greg and Brian focus on container gardening. They grow a few things in the ground, but there are limitations. For example, they can't add or remove trees to ensure proper shade and sunlight for different areas of the garden.

Container gardening, however, is much more than a dull row of plastic or terra-cotta pots. Greg and Brian enjoy finding unusual containers to house their new plants: old watering cans, a wheelbarrow, even some retired garden boots. Containers are what you make of them, they say. If you want to start a unique container garden, just take a careful look around your yard — it's most likely filled with interesting garden containers.

The back of Greg and Brian's house opens onto a large cement patio. It makes for an unusual gardening challenge. The patio is uncovered, and in summer it catches the sun's heat and bakes anything on or near it. During the hottest days, plants on the patio have to be watered twice daily. Conversely, during the winter this slab seems to hold onto the cold. Sacramento rarely freezes, but gardeners here can expect around a dozen frosty mornings in a normal year. Plants on or near this cement slab are more susceptible to the frost that this garden occasionally experiences.

However, even with all the problems this patio creates, Greg and Brian do admit a grudging appreciation for it. The idea of hiding this slab of concrete with potted plants was the initial impetus for starting their gardening project. And once they started gardening, they became addicted — and there's no cure in sight.

"Plants are our connection to Mother Earth."

— *Greg Howes*

△ The view from the back patio shows the multitude of containers Greg and Brian have put to use in their garden.

In hindsight there are a couple of things these young men would do differently were they to begin this garden over again. Brian suggests that starting with bigger pots would have been better. Early in the process of creating this herb garden, he found himself repotting some plants every two months.

Having limited space to work with, Greg and Brian planted this garden with the biointensive system — in which plants are closely spaced (see page 198 for more details) — in mind. The garden is a beautiful concentration of plants. They all seem to have flourished with this system, but Greg feels that maintenance would be easier if they could have better separated the plants by their needs. For example, keeping the drought-tolerant plants in a garden separate from those needing more water would have made caretaking a little easier.

As some of the perennial herbs that started in pots on the patio have moved into the main garden, the number of pots on the patio has decreased. Brian and Greg have graduated from using pots to using larger containers — for example, an old garden cart and a wooden box that is 2 feet by 4 feet. These larger containers add to the aesthetic appeal of the garden and make it seem less cluttered and more permanent.

Over the years the vision of this garden has changed. Originally Greg and Brian saw the garden as a visual enhancement of their outdoor living space. As they have delved into the culinary and medicinal herbs, their view of the garden has grown to include its utilitarian possibilities as well. Now the garden is an integral part of their lives; it provides not only beauty but also healing and nutrition.

When they started gardening, Greg and Brian took pleasure in sitting back in lounge chairs and enjoying the beauty of their garden from a distance. Now they find their greatest appreciation of the garden when they are working in it, when their hands are in the soil. When they are tending the garden, all their senses are at work. The fingers feel the lush fecundity of the soil, the eyes see the beauty of the plants, the nose detects exotic fragrances, and the ears hear the gentle buzz of the insects. The mind is drawn in to the natural completeness of the garden ecosystem.

For Greg Howes and Brian Fikes, the garden is a respite from their workday world. It is their connection to reality. They work in a totally artificial world; enclosed in a steel-and-concrete fortress, breathing air-conditioned air, they are cut off from nature during the day. In the evenings and on weekends they have their garden to reconnect them to a more natural way of living. Time spent in the garden rejuvenates their spirit and their souls; it is akin to meditation.

A water nymph overlooks a small pool.

Pictured on pages 128–129: Through careful planning and a fair share of creativity, Greg and Brian have created a country landscape in their small city yard.

◁ Nasturtiums, echinacea, calendula, and other herbs surround a statue of Kwan Yin, the Chinese goddess of healing. The serene gaze of the peaceful statue contrasts wonderfully with the exuberant display of bright and colorful flowers.

Greg and Brian's City Garden

GARDEN FEATURES

A Back patio herb and flower garden with birdbath

B Kwan Yin goddess shrine planted with ferns and flowers

C Raised railroad-tie bed for herbs

D Half-barrel water garden

E Tea and fragrance garden

F Cherry tree

G Chicken coop

H Grapefruit tree

I Apricot tree

J Catalpa tree

K Italian cypress underplanted with shade-loving herbs

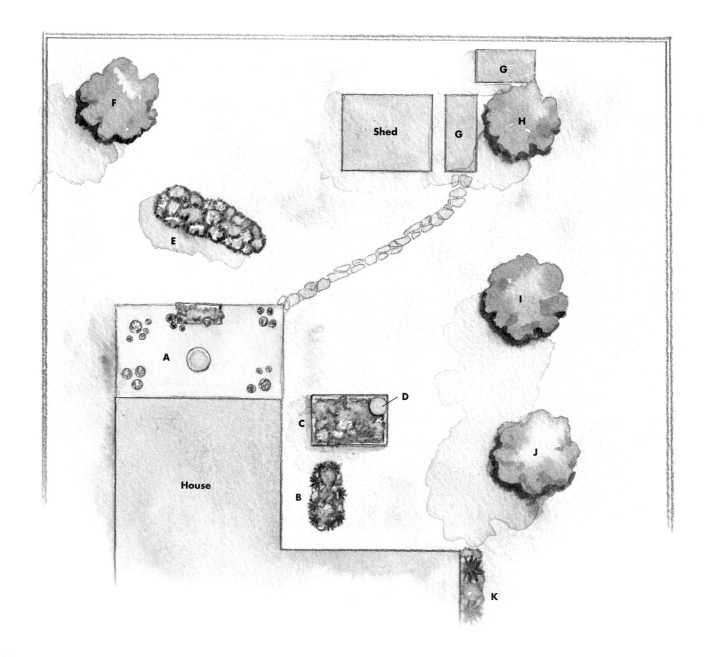

Zinnias and alyssum on the patio

Harvesting nasturtiums from the raised bed

A well-dressed scarecrow

The Kwan Yin goddess shrine in the evening

Container-grown sage

Greg and Brian's Favorite Herbs

Greg and Brian name peppermint, nasturtium, and lavender as their favorite herbs. Lavender is profiled on page 116; peppermint and nasturtium follow.

Peppermint

We were glad to hear that peppermint is at the top of Greg and Brian's list of favorite herbs. Peppermint is a refreshing, invigorating herb that should be part of every garden. When we give tours of Dry Creek Herb Farm to schoolchildren, the peppermint patch is always a favorite stop. Kids crush the leaves and exclaim, "Candy canes!"

Traditional Medicinal Uses

The strong flavor of peppermint comes mostly from its volatile oil, which also makes it a highly effective carminative (relieves gas). Gas can cause horrible abdominal pains, and a cup of peppermint tea gives quick, effective relief. Peppermint is also an invigorating nervine — some people prefer this herb over lavender for headaches. A bath infused with peppermint (using the leaves in a bath bag) is wonderfully refreshing and an excellent remedy for colds and sinus headaches.

Growing and Harvesting

Take heed of the old saying "Plant mint and stand back." This herb is an explorer that loves to creep out and send its roots everywhere. It will easily conquer the rich, loose soil of a raised bed, and if not carefully monitored, mint could be the *only* herb in your garden. In a shady, contained bed with adequate water, peppermint forms a beautiful dark green mound that will share its fragrance gleefully, whether someone has brushed by it or the cats or dogs have run through it. Smelling it like that, unexpectedly, always makes us smile.

There are ways to enjoy peppermint without having it become a nuisance. Container gardening is the easy way; simply divide and repot in the fall to avoid the binding of the roots. We grow some peppermint in full sun — it really doesn't like it, but it keeps the size down. Or grow it in its favorite setting, filtered sun or shade, and then dig up the encroaching tendrils in the fall to pot and give as gifts in the spring (we hope you have a lot of friends).

In cold climates peppermint will go dormant in the winter. We cut it back to one or two leaf joints after the first frost, and then mulch heavily.

Pick peppermint leaves from spring through fall for refreshing teas or to chop up to garnish green or fruit salads.

PEPPERMINT BROWNIES

This quick and easy recipe is sure to earn rave culinary reviews!

Heat to a simmer the liquid portion (usually water or milk) of your favorite brownie recipe. Remove from heat, stir in 1 cup of chopped fresh peppermint leaves, cover, and steep 10 minutes. Then uncover, let cool, add the liquid and mint to the rest of the mix, and bake.

Peppermint *Mentha x piperita*
Plant Cycle: Perennial,
Zones 4–9
Propagation: Mint starts easily
from root divisions or cuttings.
Parts Used: Aerial parts

Nasturtium

Nasturtium is another of Greg and Brian's favorite herbs, as it is ours. One of our fondest vacation memories is a leisurely walk we took along the cliffs of the famous ocean city of La Jolla, in southern California. The sun was warm and bright, sparkling off the blue-green water. To make the picture even more vividly beautiful, a glorious carpet of green leaves cascaded over the tops of the cliffs with ornaments of vibrant orange, scarlet, and yellow flowers. This is nasturtium in its glory.

Traditional Medicinal Uses

Like arugula, another zippy salad green, nasturtium is considered to be an aphrodisiac. Its spicy flavor certainly feels rejuvenating! The flowers, leaves, and seeds are said to have antimicrobial properties, especially in relation to the respiratory system.

"We always plant our old rusted wheelbarrow with a mixture of nasturtiums every spring. They're great because they bloom until frost and the flowers are delicious in salads and for garnish."

— *Greg Howes*

Growing and Harvesting

The lucky folks of milder climates are able to have nasturtiums all year round, with blossoms from early spring until late fall. In colder regions this colorful display is limited to the warmer months.

Nasturtium seeds are large and tough, and we usually soak them overnight before planting. However, you do want to be careful not to overwater them once planted, as the seeds can rot. Indeed, for nasturtiums and all other plants, moderation and intuition are important aspects of the art of cultivation.

In climates where the summers are hot and dry, plant nasturtiums in a spot with partial shade or filtered sun. In cooler areas, plant them in full sun or partial shade. Intermix the cheery flowers with your vegetables and salad greens for easy harvesting at dinnertime. You can also plant them sporadically around your yard or garden for eye-catching splashes of color.

There are two types of nasturtiums: a trailing variety that can be grown on the ground or staked to climb to about 6 feet tall, and a dwarf compact plant that grows only 15 inches high. The dwarf variety does well in pots.

Nasturtium leaves and flowers have a hot, snappy flavor. Add them fresh to green salads, potato salads, and pasta dishes. Adventurous cooks can harvest the tight flower buds and pickle them as a tasty substitute for capers.

◁ Fresh nasturtium flowers add spice and color to an ordinary garden salad.

the green farmacy garden

Dr. James Duke is a widely acclaimed researcher, herbalist, and author. We would need several pages simply to list his outstanding achievements in the fields of botany, ethnobotanical research, herbalism, and education. Dr. Duke's six-acre "farmette" in Fulton, Maryland, includes eighty theme gardens, each containing plants particular to the treatment of a specific disease. He uses the gardens as his outdoor classroom, mainly to educate professionals from the medical community. Dr. Duke also leads trips into the jungles of South America that focus on the ecology and culture of the Amazonian rain forest.

◁ Dr. Duke's intentions for and attentions to his gardens have manifested in a green haven rich in both beauty and utility.

Jim Duke is something of a Renaissance man. He is a clinical herbalist, renowned ethnobotanist, former researcher for the United States Department of Agriculture, author, poet, and musician. Herbalists and students of the plant kingdom know him to be one of the world's foremost authorities on medicinal herbs. His book *The Green Pharmacy* is a fixture in most herbalists' libraries. He is an amazing and multi-talented person.

We know Dr. Duke to be wise, gracious, and hospitable — a true southern gentleman. Spending time with Jim and his wife, Peggy, is an inspiration in countless ways. They feel a great commitment to each other and to all the life around them, and they are wonderful role models for all people lucky enough to meet them.

Dr. Duke's love for plants began when he was a child. Some of his earliest memories are of visits to his grandfather's farm and his uncle's nursery, where he and his "country cousins" explored the forests and fields near the Cahaba and Koosa Rivers outside Birmingham, Alabama. His mother was a gardener, and she taught Jim to love and respect plants and the wild(er) kingdom.

Many of us as children had in our neighborhoods that one person who kept to himself. Our parents told us he was "eccentric," but we thought he was just plain weird, and we avoided him. But instead of shying away from *his* neighbor, Jim befriended him, and in so doing he tapped into a wealth of information.

It was "Old Mr. Brooks" who introduced a young Jim Duke to the idea of eating "weeds." The elder neighbor and the young boy took long walks in the nearby woods, and the child learned many lessons about wild foods. There he first sampled plants such as chestnut and watercress, which to this day remain a part of Dr. Duke's dinner-table fare.

Jim Duke's first summer job was at Umstead State Park in North Carolina. It was his good fortune to be paid to do the things he loved: hiking, camping, canoeing, and taking stock of plants and animals. While cataloging and recording his observations of this wild place, Jim began learning how to live off the land, knowledge that would serve him well years later in the jungles of South America.

During his teenage years, Jim's love of music grew. He was a skilled guitarist and bass player; when he was sixteen, he even cut a 78 record in Nashville. The music director at the University of North Carolina urged him to attend the campus there in Chapel Hill as a music major. Jim agreed. But as much as he enjoyed music, Jim's first calling was botany, and he soon changed his major.

Christmas fern

"Gardening is a wonderful way to slow the aging process. It offers five benefits useful in maintaining youth and vigor: exercise, fresh air, relaxation, sunshine (but not too much!), and communion with nature and nature's herbs."

— James Duke

◁ The asthma garden features coltsfoot and anise hyssop, classic herbs for the treatment of respiratory conditions. In the background, you can see the bright blossoms of chamomile and feverfew that mark the allergy garden.

△ The white blooms of valerian rise high over its green foliage.

Dr. Duke has had many interesting and unusual projects over the years, including studying the possible use of fungi in biological warfare and investigating alternative crops for growers of narcotic plants in the tropics. One of his earliest projects was studying different species of the carrot family in Mexico. He fell in love with Latin America and has returned many times to study its culture and botanical world.

When Jim travels he always prefers to "go native," feeling this is a much better way to get to know an area and its people. As he became acquainted with the people of Latin America, they began to teach him about the uses of the plants in their forests. On one expedition to Panama, he contracted a case of salmonella poisoning. After many prescriptions from Western doctors failed, he tried the local plant medicines and found his first relief. He was sold. As he says in *The Green Pharmacy,* "If we all give herbal medicines the chance they deserve, botanical medicine will spread like kudzu, and the world will be better for it."

After a long, rewarding career spent traveling the world studying plants and identifying and learning their attributes, Jim began sharing the wisdom he had gathered from the indigenous herbalists he met. In the late 1990s he went on a number of "ecotours," guiding tourists through the jungles of South and Central America and introducing them to the many beneficial plants inhabiting these wild places.

Now, during what James Duke calls his "sunrise years," he is devoting his energy to trying to raise awareness of herbal alternatives to pharmaceutical medicines. Gardening, which he has always loved, has become an essential part of this worthy effort. The six-acre "farmette" that Dr. Duke calls home is his opportunity to play with, experiment with, and teach about the herbs and plants he has grown to love during his illustrious career. The plan for his garden is a bit different from that of most gardeners. The layout includes eighty different garden plots; each section contains herbs for a specific ailment, such as cancer, diabetes, bronchitis, and depression. Doctors regularly come for tours of the gardens, and there they are introduced to some of the healing herbs James Duke has studied, used, and loved over the years — and that he feels will be proved effective as treatments.

STARTING YOUR OWN GREEN FARMACY GARDEN

We've noticed that different families have their own particular health issues. Some families get colds often. Some easily catch flus or sore throats. Headaches can be a problem for another, and some are prone to bumps, bruises, and breaks. Whether it is their environment, their lifestyle, or their genetic makeup, we often see one prominent health profile per family.

Study your family and see what are the most common ailments. Then research herbs that are helpful in prevention and healing of those problems. There are often many herbs to choose from for each issue. Then take some time to narrow down the herbs to those that will grow well in your area.

Plant this "farmacy" garden close to your house for easy access. While the plants are growing, sit with them, watch them in their various cycles, and learn what they have to say. You will want to read books or take classes on proper harvesting and preparation of these plants.

Here are some suggestions for herbs for specific farmacy gardens.

Allergy Garden
Chamomile
Feverfew
Garlic
Ginkgo
Horseradish
Stinging nettle

Heart Garden
Borage
Ginkgo
Hawthorn tree
Linden tree
Motherwort
Yarrow

Cancer Garden
Birch tree
Bloodroot
Calendula
Celandine
Echinacea
Garlic
Huang qi
Licorice
May apple
Periwinkle
Stillingia
Turmeric
Winged bean
Yew

Headache Garden
Feverfew
Lavender
Meadowsweet
Peppermint
Rosemary
Skullcap
Wood betony

Respiratory Garden
Angelica
Coltsfoot
Elecampane
Hyssop
Marsh mallow
Mullein
Thyme

Each of the eighty gardens is marked with a carved stone.

△ Multitiered terraces allow Dr. Duke to garden on what is otherwise very steeply sloping land. Staircases cut through the gardens allow visitors to climb from one level to the next. At the very bottom lies a small garden pond.

Just below Jim and Peggy's house, spread over four terraces, is the Green Farmacy Garden, the eighty garden plots that address most of the major health concerns of humankind, ranging from cancer to baldness to kidney stones. A local landscaper whose wife had gone on ecotours with Dr. Duke to Maine and Peru helped with the initial design of the garden.

Since there were fairly steep slopes in the area that was to become the garden, Dr. Duke decided to build terraces. Each of the four terraces he installed now contains roughly twenty garden plots, and the lower levels also feature a bog garden, a lotus pool, and a small waterfall spilling into a quiet pond.

One of the major hindrances to the project was the rocky nature of the soil on the property — at one time this property had been called Stony Hill. It took Dr. Duke and his helpers quite a bit of time and effort to remove the larger rocks and amend the soil on the terraces. One rock alone cost a thousand dollars to remove and break into smaller pieces.

Water is also a challenge for Dr. Duke's garden, as it is for many. Recent years have seen some of the worst droughts on record, which sorely taxed the wells and water resources on this property. In the future Jim hopes to put in a deeper well and erect a storage dam, which will establish self-sustainability for the gardens.

▽ Because his gardens feature herbs sharing a common affinity for a specific ailment, Dr. Duke occasionally has to grow plants in an environment not optimal for them. For example, in one sunny garden he wanted to grow shade-loving ginseng and goldenseal. So he constructed little umbrellas for the plants, and now they grow happily under their protective parasols, like southern belles strolling on a summer day.

Pictured on pages 144–145: White-flowering elder, pink echinacea, and quiet goldenseal under its bamboo shelter are overshadowed by a vibrant patch of lavender.

Dr. Duke has spent much of his life observing nature: its habits, its preferences, its ways. The results of these studies have all had a hand in the planning of his gardens. The ranch-style house sits above the formal Green Farmacy Garden. Below that is a forested, fern-laden valley now called Yin Yang Yuan.

This more wild portion of the gardens is Dr. Duke's favorite part of the property. At one time he called it Phenology Valley. *Phenology* is the study of the timing, or the sequencing, of events in the lives of plants and animals. In the Yin Yang Yuan Valley, there is a phenological march, a "green parade of life," passing right before his eyes throughout the calendar year. As different plants emerge in the spring, the timing of their budding and blooming is based in part on the weather of that particular winter, in part on the plants' genetic makeup, and in part on factors that we do not yet know or understand. Men like Dr. Duke are spending countless hours in observation hoping to learn more of the secrets of phenology.

One of the reasons for the name change to Yin Yang Yuan is the topogra-

phy of the land. One side of the valley is a colder, north-facing "yin" slope, and the other side is a warmer, south-facing "yang" slope. On average the south-facing yang slope flowers and fruits about two weeks before the north yin slope (a demonstration of phenology).

Dr. Duke has planted so that something in Yin Yang Yuan Valley is in flower every month of the year. He has a stunning Christmas rose that flowers from December through March. In the fall he has flowering witch hazel, which blooms in October. But to Dr. Duke the most exciting flowers are those that herald the coming of spring's rejuvenation: the cultivated crocuses opening around Groundhog Day, followed closely by a rush of wildflowers, many of which are medicinal — all of them proselytizing their benefits with their beautiful colors and shapes.

The Yin Yang Yuan Valley is an ongoing experiment for the good doctor of botany. He has taken cuttings from many plants and planted them on the yin side of the valley, then taken more cuttings from those same plants and planted them on the yang side of the valley. Having the two distinctive environments directly facing each other gives Dr. Duke the opportunity to test close at hand different growing conditions and to understand how these environments affect the growth patterns of the various plants.

◁ Dr. Duke spends countless hours deep in thought in a chair at the edge of Yin Yang Yuan, observing the phenology of his own little corner of creation.

Although he is now in his seventies, Dr. Duke's enthusiasm for gardening has not waned. A man with a great intellectual curiosity, he continues to be fascinated by the botanical world. He considers the living green things to be his metaphorical mates, and he describes his time spent with them in the Yin Yang Yuan Valley as rejuvenating and life extending. For Dr. James Duke, the plant kingdom is a world's worth of wonder and awe — and his life's love.

◁ *Insane Libido*, carved and shaped from black walnut by the late Bob Howard, a friend of Dr. Duke, symbolizes the interplay between yin and yang, male and female, in the garden. Its form suggests the intertwining of beautiful male and female bodies holding tight in their embrace but still metaphorically questioning the meaning of coexistence: Are we one? Are we two? Are we any at all? Strangely enough, Bee and Bop, a pair of goats that used to live in the Yin Yang Yuan Valley, took a great liking to this piece of art and often played, grazed, and napped near it.

Dr. Duke's
Green Farmacy Garden

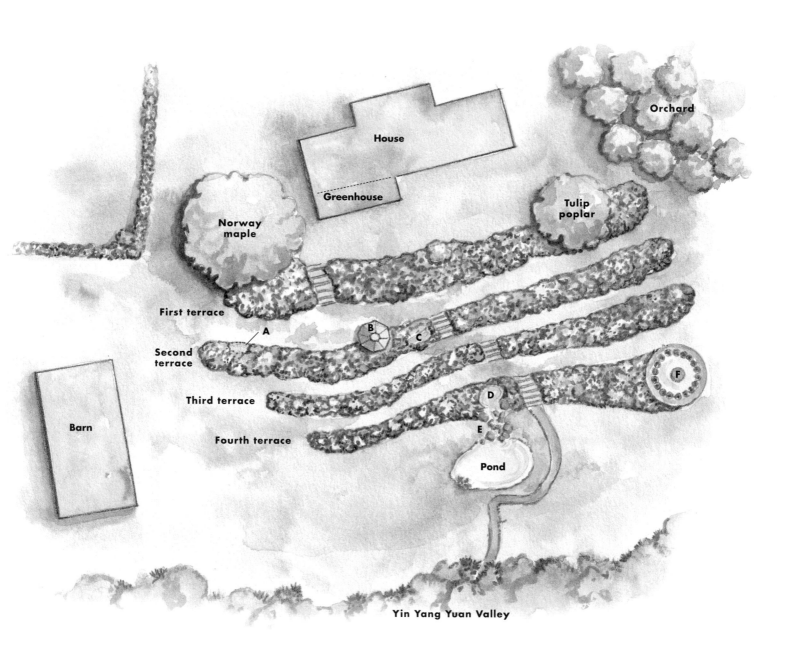

Orchard

House

Greenhouse

Norway
maple

Tulip
poplar

First terrace

A

B

C

Second
terrace

Third terrace

D

E

F

Fourth terrace

Barn

Pond

Yin Yang Yuan Valley

GARDEN FEATURES

A Peat bog

B Gazebo

C Lotus pond

D Filter marsh

E Waterfall

F Floral clock

The first terrace contains aphrodisia, baldness, prostate, dysmenorrhea, endometriosis, breast health, menopause, PMS, aging, Alzheimer's, vertigo, glaucoma, thyroid, liver, maculitis, osteoporosis, tinnitus, ulcer, wrinkle, and Parkinson's gardens.

The second terrace contains cancer, leukemia, angina, heartburn, heart disease, diabetes, obesity, addiction, attention-deficit disorder, carpal tunnel syndrome, high blood pressure, chronic fatigue syndrome, depression, fibromyalgia, insomnia, multiple sclerosis, smoking, and psoriasis gardens.

The third terrace contains arthritis, gout, allergy, asthma, bronchitis, bursitis, backache, headache, toothache, cystitis, diverticulitis, dermatitis, inflammatory bowel disease, laryngitis, sinusitis, vaginitis, yeast infection, constipation, diarrhea, and dyspopsia gardens.

The fourth terrace contains kidney stone, varicosis, bruises, burns, cuts, earache, fever, hangover, bacteria, cold and flu, fungal infection, immune system, herpes, HIV and viral infection, and insect-repellent gardens.

The gazebo on the second terrace

A bright spot of lavender on an otherwise green terrace

Vivacious echinacea

Dr. Duke's Favorite Herbs

Dr. Duke is a connoisseur of the herb world. When we asked him to pick out his three favorites, he thought carefully, then named evening primrose, fennel, and passionflower.

Evening Primrose

If you plan on growing evening primrose in your garden, you'd better like it — a lot! Easily started from seed and not picky about soil conditions, this tall "weed" will sprout up all over the garden.

The first year the plant appears as an attractive, large, low-growing rosette of leaves. In its second spring, a tall central flower stalk rises up from the middle of the rosette. True to its name, each evening two perfect, four-petaled blossoms open. If you have the patience, sit by the plant at dusk, watching carefully. Slowly but irrepressibly, the blossoms open before your eyes. It is a rare glimpse of nature's subtle beauty and magic.

The next morning, after their one night of glory, these flowers close and die. In the evening they are replaced by two new blossoms farther up the stalk. The spent flowers give rise to pods that hold numerous tiny seeds. When mature, the pods turn brown and split, dropping the seeds to the ground, or into the hand of an herbalist ready to eat them.

Traditional Medicinal Uses

Evening primrose seeds are a tremendous source of GLA (gamma linolenic acid), an important essential fatty acid. Oil extracted from evening primrose seeds is often sold as a health supplement. It can be used for a variety of reproductive system problems specific to women. A nice side effect is that it often improves the condition of the skin.

There is much active research on the connection between a lack of essential fatty acids in the diet, such as GLA, and certain diseases. Supplementing the diet with GLA may improve inflammatory conditions, diabetes, and arthritis.

Evening primrose also contains small amounts of tryptophan, an amino acid known as an aid to sound sleep.

Growing and Harvesting

We never planted the evening primrose that grows abundantly on our farm. It just showed up in our flower garden several years ago and has been around ever since. To grow evening primrose, in fall or early spring simply scatter seeds carelessly about — really! In warmer climates, the seeds may require cold stratification.

The first-year root is edible, which is good to know because you'll probably want to thin out the plants. Eat it raw — it has a slightly hot tang, like a radish.

To harvest the seeds, wait until much of the stalk is full of mature brown seedpods on the verge of bursting open. Shake the stalk over a cloth laid on the ground, or carefully cut the stalks and shake them inside paper bags to release the seeds.

Dr. Duke recommends eating the seeds by using them in your food as you would poppy seeds. They make a great addition to bread recipes: Mix ground seeds in with the dough or sprinkle them on top of the crust. Or grind the seeds with olive oil, store the blend in the refrigerator, and use it in salad dressings and other recipes.

EVENING PRIMROSE *OENOTHERA BIENNIS*
Plant Cycle: Biennial, Zones 4–8
Propagation: Evening primrose is easily started from seed.
Parts Used: Aerial parts

Fennel

We were pleased to hear that fennel is another of Dr. Duke's favorite herbs. Here in California, fennel lines freeways and dirt roads, decorates empty lots, and inhabits unused portions of farm-land. If ever we leave our home state, a simple sniff of fennel's licorice-like scent is enough to send us "California Dreaming."

To the Celts and Anglo-Saxons, fennel's stateliness and affinity for the sun signaled its ability to impart long life, courage, and virility to its users. It was also gathered ritually to hang above doorways for protection of the home.

Tall, green, and lush, this noble herb has been used in food and medicines for centuries. The seeds are both medicine and confection, and its fragrant, yellow, umbrella like blossoms add a touch of class to any flower arrangement.

Traditional Medicinal Uses

Used for centuries by many cultures as a carminative (aids digestion), fennel seeds are often found on dinner tables in Indian homes; Ayurvedic practitioners recommend chewing three to six seeds after a meal to improve digestion. In our herb shop we sell old-fashioned candy tins holding candy-coated fennel seeds, which were perhaps the nation's first breath fresheners. We also often use fennel seeds in teas to hide the taste of more resinous respiratory herbs.

Fennel seeds have antispasmodic properties and may be helpful with digestive spasms. By eating fennel seeds, a nursing mother can ease her baby's colic. Fennel also has an affinity with the respiratory system and in the past was often used as an ingredient for homemade cough syrups.

According to well-known herbalist Steven Foster, a tea made from the leaves has been shown to produce a significant reduction in arterial blood pressure without affecting the heart or respiratory rate. The seed decocted and strained as a tea can also be used as an eyewash for sore or inflamed eyes.

Growing and Using

Because of its Mediterranean origins, fennel can tolerate drought conditions and survive in even the poorest soil. It prefers full sun.

All parts of this common fennel are useful; however, there are subspecies and varieties that are grown more specifically for certain plant parts. *Foeniculum vulgare* 'Rubrum', also known as bronze fennel, is grown for its beautiful copper foliage, which makes an attractive garnish that decorates the plates of the finest restaurants. The finocchio or Florence fennel *(F. vulgare* var. *azoricum)* has thick stalks and a bulbous rootstock that is deliciously succulent eaten raw or cooked. The common fresh fennel leaves can be finely chopped and added to fruit salads or to sweet yogurt dressings to adorn them. It can also be added to green salads and their oil-and-vinegar dressings. We've added the chopped fresh leaves to other steamed greens and to Italian and Greek sauces. The root of the common fennel may be eaten also, raw or cooked, but it is not quite as tasty as the finocchio.

Fennel is high in potassium, iron, and vitamin C. One cup of fennel contains 60 percent of the RDA of vitamin A.

FENNEL *FOENICULUM VULGARE*
Plant Cycle: Perennial,
Zones 4–9
Propagation: Fennel is
easily started from seed.
Parts Used: Seeds,
leaves, and roots

Passionflower

Dr. Duke also asked that we profile passionflower as one of his favorite herbs. Although the "passion" in passionflower refers to the passion of Christ, the sensuous spectacle of this flower would startle anyone. Clinging vines can slither up to heights of 20 feet, and in summer the seductive purple-and-white flowers give a glorious show.

Traditional Medicinal Uses

Passionflower is best known for its sedative and sleep-inducing properties. It has an affinity with hops, another herb used to treat insomnia. Here at Dry Creek Herb Farm, that duo is the basis for our best-selling sleep tea.

Older herbals of the eclectic era list passionflower as being antispasmodic and useful for general seizures. There are herbalists today who use this herb as an aid for epilepsy and Parkinson's disease. Passionflower is also helpful in lowering blood pressure and is used in combination with other circulatory herbs.

Growing and Harvesting

Passionflower is native to the southeastern United States, where it thrives in well-drained, moderately fertile soils. It likes both sunny places and partial shade as long as there is moisture and humidity and not a lot of wind.

In cooler climates, passionflower will want full sun. In warmer climates, give it partial shade. The vine does die back in winter, after the first frost.

The species *Passiflora incarnata* is probably the most hardy of the *Passiflora* genus, but even it will not tolerate severe winters. Herbalists intent on growing passionflower where it is not hardy can grow it as an annual, planting it out each spring after the last frost. Save seeds through the winter by wrapping them in peat moss, or take cuttings and root them in a greenhouse over the winter. Of course, you can also grow it all year long in a greenhouse or on a warm, sunny windowsill.

Harvest the leaves and flowers when the plant is in full bloom.

DEEP SLEEP TEA

For restful sleep, try a deep sleep tea or bath before bedtime.

1½ parts dried chamomile flowers
1 part dried skullcap leaf
½ part dried passionflower
 (leaf and flower)
½ part dried hops strobiles
½ part dried lavender blossoms
½ part dried mint leaves

Blend all ingredients. To make a tea, use 1 teaspoon of this blend per 1 cup of water. Bring the water to a boil, pour over the herbs, cover, and let steep 10 minutes. Strain before drinking.

This blend may also be used as a bath soak before bedtime. Make 2 quarts of tea as described above, using 2 teaspoons of the blend per cup of water. Strain and add to the bathwater.

PASSIONFLOWER *PASSIFLORA INCARNATA*
Plant Cycle: Perennial, Zones 6–9
Propagation: Passionflower is best
started from cuttings. Keep indoors
until well rooted and until all danger
of frost has passed.
Parts Used: Aerial parts

Ravenhill Farm

a jewel by the sea

Andrew Yeoman and Nöel Richardson threw off the cloak of corporate city life twenty-two years ago and moved to the country to become herb farmers. A complementary pair, one serves up patience, with feet firmly planted on the earth, while the other is a visionary, full of ideas and eagerness. This balance of yin and yang is reflected in their gardens and their business. Situated in a most romantic setting on Vancouver Island in British Columbia, Ravenhill Farm is an herbal paradise born of hard work. In addition to gardening and teaching classes at the farm, both Andrew and Nöel are published authors of herb growing and cooking books, and both write regularly for several magazines.

◁ Ravenhill Farm stands on the lower slopes of the beautiful green, rolling hills on the Saanich Peninsula of Vancouver Island. The friendly inhabitants of this area include Ravenhill owners Andrew Yeoman and Nöel Richardson as well as an array of animals and plants.

A Ravenhill Farm peacock

"Growing herbs

puts you in touch with

the earth, which can

often be a healing

experience in this busy,

stress-filled life."

— *Nöel Richardson*

One of the jewels of our earthly paradise is Ravenhill Farm, the home and livelihood of Nöel Richardson and Andrew Yeoman. Ravenhill is located on the Saanich Peninsula on Vancouver Island in British Columbia. Our first visit to the farm was on one of those near-perfect days that are so common to the area. The temperature was warm, not hot; the sky was blue with an aesthetic arrangement of soft white cumulus clouds. We sat on a stone-and-thyme bench and held hands, soaking up the romantic ambience. We could see the blue waters of the ocean framed by the rolling Saanich hills covered in lush grasses, trees, and an assortment of wildflowers, and off in the distance we could even see snow-covered mountains. We have loved Ravenhill ever since.

The beauty of Ravenhill reflects

Nöel and Andrew's love for each other and for this piece of land. Nöel and Andrew moved to Ravenhill in 1979, in search of a lifestyle that would bring them closer to the earth. Andrew needed a break from working in the office towers of Calgary, and Nöel wanted to pursue her love of herbs and cooking. They found a ten-acre parcel with a gently sloping southern aspect in Saanichton on Vancouver Island, just thirty minutes from the city of Victoria.

Once the land was acquired, the challenge for Andrew and Nöel was to determine exactly how to proceed. Though they work well together, they have different approaches to life. Nöel is full of ideas and enthusiasm; she was ready to till the soil and get herbs in the ground right away. Andrew is the more cautious type; he wanted to observe the site for a period and get to know the rhythms of the land and its environment. As with all successful marriages, a balance was struck and work began.

With a cautious approach they started to build the gardens. Trying to keep within a budget, they began and completed one project at a time. In this way the garden grew at a slow, natural pace. The work kept Nöel's eagerness satisfied; the schedule satisfied Andrew's desire to observe and get to know the land as it revealed its secrets in a natural rhythm.

Ravenhill's soil is a fast-draining, thin clay loam with many granite outcrops. Soil testing revealed the need for adding lime or dolomite to counter the inherent acidity. Because of the thin layer of soil and the gentle slopes of the property, Andrew and Nöel terraced the gardens and built up the bed walls to deepen the soil. They filled the beds with compost made with the help of their chickens and sheep. Some of the "less greedy" herbs, such as thyme, grew very well on the property's original soil with little amending needed. Now, each October, Nöel and Andrew cover the beds with a green winter manure or cover crop and in the spring add more compost and other organic materials to the beds.

▷ A bed of salvia lines the red-tiled pathway that runs through the center of Ravenhill Farm.

All gardeners know that without water there is no garden. When Andrew and Nöel purchased the Ravenhill property, the house and garden were supported by only a poor well and a small irrigation pond. They drilled a new 500-foot well, but it produced not even a dribble. Discouraged but undaunted, they drilled another well, this time to only 300 feet. There they found water, although not quite what they had hoped for. At times this well produces just 4 gallons per minute, which is adequate for a home and small garden but not quite enough for a large production garden.

The water situation forced Nöel and Andrew to rethink their farming plan. They decided to concentrate on herbs suitable to dry conditions. Fortunately, many of the popular Mediterranean culinary herbs — rosemary, thyme, and basil, for example — fall into this category.

For two years Nöel and Andrew prepared their soil, planted seeds, and read as many gardening books as they could lay their hands on. When they felt that they were growing enough herbs to sell, they approached a number of local restaurants.

Within five years they were selling fresh-cut herbs to more than twenty restaurants.

The business of supplying herbs to the restaurant industry was very successful, and eventually they built a greenhouse to extend their season and hired help to keep up with the workload. But success usually has its price, and Nöel and Andrew found themselves away from their beloved farm all too often. This was not the lifestyle they had sought when they first moved to Saanichton. They realized that, for them, smaller was better. They decided to cut back on the restaurant deliveries and open the gardens to the public on Sundays from April to October to sell herb plants.

The decision to make their gardens more public changed their business and lives in many ways. As word got out, visitors from all around came to view the gardens. Andrew and Nöel were invited to speak at venues such as garden clubs and garden shows. Group tours for chefs in training, gardeners, and landscape architects became popular. And Ravenhill began to host the Art-in-the-Barn Craft Fair, a grand exhibition of the work of local artists and crafters, once a year.

Pictured on pages 162–163: A gray santolina hedge (lower left) borders the path that flows past a small formal herb garden (on the left) and shrubs and perennial beds (on the right).

◁ A recently harvested bundle of fennel attracts a curious Ravenhill Farm cat.

Most gardeners revel in those small magic moments inherent to garden life. A favorite flower luxuriant in the morning dew, a striking pink-purple sunset reflected in the garden pond, the first sight of new, tender sprouts in the spring — all these are important for the spirit.

But occasionally extraordinary events take place in the garden that leave their mark for all to see. One such event took place at Ravenhill on a drizzly day a number of years ago. A young Salish carver, Aubrey La Fortune, had created a totem pole, and an unveiling was held at Ravenhill, attended by friends and the family of the artist. When the artist saw his work standing tall in the mist that covered that beautiful garden, he shed tears of joy. Ravenhill is now blessed with three of his carvings.

Andrew and Nöel have carved for themselves the life that they want. The original idea had been to find a piece of land from which they could make their living by growing culinary herbs and selling them to the restaurant industry. The plan was slightly altered when they opened the gardens to the public. Then Nöel's writing career took off. Now Andrew is a published author, also, and they both write for several magazines.

They see for themselves a future of more of the same: tending their gardens, welcoming fellow gardeners to enjoy the beauty they have created, writing about the things they love, and waiting for their next inspiration. For them, these are the things that make a quality life.

A totem pole carved by Aubrey La Fortune; from top to bottom, three chiefs, the Raven of Ravenhill, and the Frog, whose spring song brings the winter dances to a close

▷ Ravenhill's gardens are open to the public on Sundays from April through July

Andrew and Nöel's Ravenhill Farm

GARDEN FEATURES

A Herb tables
B Herb and vegetable bed
C View over Saanich Inlet
D Greenhouse
E Gray santolina hedge
F Thyme bench
G Small formal herb garden
H Blackberry bushes
I Totem pole
J Thyme hill

K Garage/shop for herb sales
L Leaf mold bins
M Paddock for sheep and geese
N Goose pond

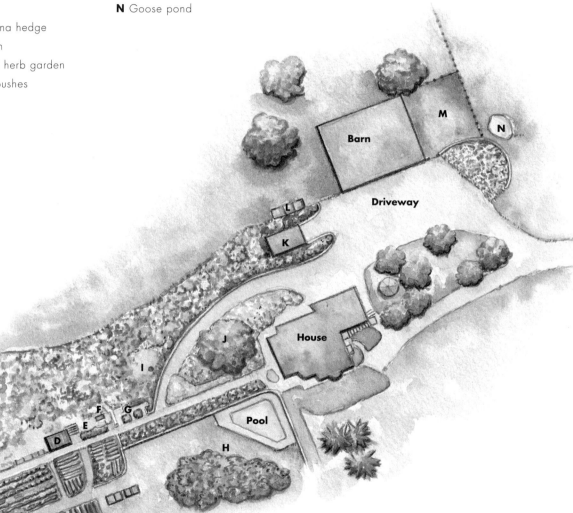

Lamb's ears, chives, and geraniums in the herb bed

Thyme bench

David Crone, an employee, in front of the garage/shop

Greenhouse

Gray santolina hedge

Andrew and Nöel's Favorite Herbs

As cooks and restaurant herb suppliers, Andrew and Nöel favor culinary herbs. The three herbs that top their list of favorites are tarragon, basil, and rosemary. We've profiled rosemary on page 58; tarragon and basil follow.

Tarragon

Tarragon has a light, licorice-like flavor. It is a staple in fines herbes and is essential for the classic Béarnaise sauce. It also makes a wonderful seasoning for poultry, eggs, and veal.

Traditional Medicinal Uses

Herbals from the 1800s speak of tarragon as a general tonic useful to the heart, liver, and digestion; some describe tarragon as useful for "women's problems." However, most modern herbals do not list medicinal uses for tarragon. The exception is Dr. Duke's *Green Pharmacy*. He cites tarragon as helpful for amenorrhea (irregular menstrual cycles). He also notes that tarragon contains six compounds that lower blood pressure.

In the Garden

Tarragon is a perennial herb that needs a cold winter to bring out its best flavor the following spring. Because tarragon goes completely dormant in winter, and in some locations dies back considerably, many new, unknowing herb gardeners pull it up, thinking it dead. If only they had waited patiently until spring to see the first green sprigs pop up with a promise of gourmet dishes!

Tarragon prefers well-drained soil and lots of sun. It is easy to grow and will spread itself over more territory each year. A first-year plant, depending on climate and soil, will grow to 12 to 18 inches in diameter. Nöel cautions that although tarragon can be grown in a container, it wants a lot of root space. Restricted roots, she warns, can cause the plant to lose much of its flavor. Many herb-gardening experts recommend digging up and dividing tarragon every three years. Cut back and mulch well in the winter to protect the roots from frost.

We begin to harvest our tarragon in early summer. Although we trim it back about two thirds, it grows back even stronger. If we manage a plant properly, we can get four or five harvests per growing season.

NÖEL'S CREAMY TARRAGON DRESSING

This delicious dressing is adapted from Nöel's cookbook *Simple Delights*.

    1 cup mayonnaise
    ½ cup milk
    ¼ cup vegetable oil
    2 tablespoons white wine vinegar
    2 cloves garlic, peeled and crushed
    2 tablespoons finely chopped tarragon
    ½ teaspoon curry powder

Put all the ingredients in a blender or food processor and blend until smooth. Chill in the refrigerator for several hours before serving. Store in the refrigerator, where the dressing will keep for up to a week.

FRENCH TARRAGON *ARTEMISIA DRACUNCULUS* VAR. *SATIVA*

Plant Cycle: Perennial, Zones 4–7

Propagation: French tarragon must be started from root divisions. If you are offered tarragon seed, it is from Russian tarragon, a definitely inferior culinary herb.

Parts Used: Aerial parts

Basil

Ask any number of herbalists and chefs what their favorite culinary herb is and nine out of ten will say basil. Andrew and Nöel are no exception, and they asked us to feature basil as one of their favorite herbs.

Basil comes in many flavors that are used to season a vast array of dishes. Many seed catalogs sell different basil varieties together as a collection. We have seen these as "basil patches" in many gardens, where they make a colorful and fragrant display.

Pesto preparation

SHATOIYA'S EASY FOLK PESTO

Go into the garden and see what's green and in season. Gather a combination to equal about 6 cups. Remove any hard stems. Add the greens cup by cup to a whirling food processor together with about 1 cup of Parmesan cheese and about 1 cup of nuts or seeds, such as pecans, walnuts, pine nuts, almonds, sunflower seeds, and pistachios.

Add as much garlic as you want. Start with four cloves, taste, then add to your desired potency and breath tolerance. Blend in enough olive oil to get the consistency you want — we usually add anywhere between ½ and 2 cups. An oilier pesto is better as a sauce for pasta; a drier pesto is better as a spread. Store, refrigerated, in a glass jar with a tight lid. It will keep about three weeks. For long-term storage, spoon the pesto into ice-cube trays and freeze.

SUGGESTED GREENS FOR PESTO INCLUDE:

Angelica leaves (small amount)
Arugula
Basil
Chickweed
Chives
Cilantro
Dandelion leaves
French sorrel
Horseradish leaves (center stem removed)
Lamb's-quarters
Lovage leaves (small amount)
Mallow or marsh mallow leaves
Marjoram leaves (stems removed)
Miner's lettuce
Nettle leaves (stems removed)
Oregano leaves (stems removed)
Parsley
Rosemary
Spinach
Thyme leaves (stems removed)
Violet leaves

Traditional Medicinal Uses

Basil brings strength; here at Dry Creek Herb Farm, we often recommend it to people recovering from a debilitating illness. Basil also has antispasmodic properties that can alleviate digestive complaints. A tea made from basil can help the bowels move, but too much of it may cause diarrhea.

Basil's strong essential oil has a wide range of uses, but it is most notable as a tonic for the nervous system. It is said to ease headaches, anxiety, and tension and to bring clarity and strength to a fatigued mind. It also acts as a carminative, meaning that it relieves gas.

Growing and Harvesting

Basil is happy in just about any sunny garden. It also grows well in pots outdoors in partial shade or indoors on sunny windowsills. Sow the seeds or set out the seedlings after the threat of frost is gone. Choose your location carefully, as too hot a midday sun or too strong a wind can "burn" the tender leaves.

Basil seedlings are susceptible to a fungal disease called damping-off, which rots the seedlings' tiny stems. An easy preventive is to water the plants with cool nettle and chamomile tea until their first true leaves appear.

When the basil plants are bushy, it's time to begin your harvest, an event that continues all summer long. Pick the larger leaves first, leaving the small ones to grow. To extend the harvest, pinch out the flower stalks as they appear. As our growing season nears its end, we let our basil flower and go to seed, which allows us to have basil every year without doing any more than waiting for spring.

BASIL *OCIMUM* SPP.
Plant Cycle: Annual or tender perennial
Propagation: Basil is easily grown from seed.
Parts Used: Aerial parts

Caprilands

the queen mother of
herb gardens

Adelma Grenier Simmons turned a rocky, run-down, mismanaged goat farm into one of the most renowned herb gardens in North America: Caprilands Herb Farm of Coventry, Connecticut. Adelma passed on in 1997, and the gardens are now managed by her husband, Professor Edward Cook.

Caprilands is truly the "grande dame" of herb gardens. The grounds include extensive gardens, a large nursery, several herb-themed gift shops, and a dining room on the first floor of the owner's home. With its luncheons, dinners, plants, gifts, teas, and classes, Caprilands offers something for every herb enthusiast.

◁ Caprilands features an amazing array of beautiful gardens. Neatly laid paths of stepping-stones, mulch, gravel, or brick wind their way among them.

Adelma Grenier Simmons was a true visionary who predicted, more than sixty years ago, the herbal renaissance taking place in North America today. She spent much of her life educating the public in the culinary use of herbs and in the refined art of herbal fragrance and decoration. Adelma was a prolific writer, and the bookstore at Caprilands is filled with her books. Her life and her gardens at Caprilands have served as a role model for an entire generation of herbalists. Rosemary Gladstar is often given credit for rekindling North American interest in medicinal herbalism, but it is Adelma whom she cites as her inspiration.

Adelma's family purchased the fifty-acre parcel of land that was to become Caprilands in 1929. The surrounding town of Coventry, Connecticut, is a lush, green-pastured land dotted with beautiful old farmhouses. The future home of Caprilands, however, was an eyesore, the result of years of mismanagement and neglect. Adelma's family had the foresight to see what this land could become with a little imagination and a lot of work. The original idea was to turn the fifty acres into a self-sustaining farm, complete with dairy cattle, goats, pigs, and chickens. Adelma was the spark behind the vision and was willing to work hard to see it come to fruition.

It was the year of the stock market crash. In 1929, a job was a precious gift; for each job, there was more than a handful of people waiting and willing to take it. To forgo a steady income (however small) to enter the uncharted waters of self-employment was considered quite unwise. Adelma and her parents had outside jobs, and at first they tried to sustain the security of employment while building a foundation for their new self-sufficient life. They built a milkshed and began to make pot cheese and butter. But they soon found that dairy farming and tending to a variety of farm animals required more attention than they could spare while still working their "day jobs." They decided to scale back the dairy business temporarily and focus on creating gardens.

Adelma had a very strong connection with the goats, but as much as she enjoyed working with them, she found this pursuit to be less than profitable. Though she eventually changed her focus to be more involved with herbs than goats, the farm still retains the name Caprilands (Goatlands), deriving from the Latin *caper,* or "goat."

During a waning moment in Adelma's infatuation with raising goats, she stood overlooking the goat pen and came to the realization that the space would make an ideal herb garden. It was a moment of great clarity: She saw her future and the future of the land. As if struck by an arrow from her muse, from that instant Adelma knew her true purpose in her marriage to this land.

Bottle-feeding an eager young sheep

◁ At Caprilands, herbs grow everywhere, from the edges of the property all the way up to the back door of the main house.

Adelma laid the stones for the first walkways herself, and as she laid the stones she envisioned a series of small gardens, each depicting a different aspect of growing and using herbs. These smaller gardens, when linked together, would make an herb garden of grand proportions.

The land was rocky and dry, and the soil greatly depleted. But Adelma's vision showed her that this site also had lots of sun, and the soil, though poor, drained well — two prime requirements for an outstanding herb garden. She started small, with realistic goals, and the garden grew in gradual increments. The first garden, which has become the butterfly garden (named for its shape, not because it contains herbs known to draw butterflies), showcased the most important and well-known herbs of the day. Over time, Adelma created gardens to feature herbs of a particular color or for a specific use. One by one these gardens were added to the fabric of Caprilands, each adding a unique texture to the overall picture. It would take many years for Adelma's original vision to be realized — it wasn't until 1978 that the plantings conceived in her original reverie were in place.

▷ Vertical elements such as trees, shrubs, and walls lend a sense of closeness and intimacy to many of the gardens in the expansive farm.

Caprilands Herb Farm

GARDEN FEATURES

A Herbaceous Border
B Potted Garden
C Dooryard Garden
D Fragrance Garden
E Cook's Garden
F Ivy Garden
G Saint's Garden
H Garden of the Pinks
I Identification Garden
J Garden of Antique Roses
K White Border Garden
L Herb & Vegetable Garden
M Strawberry Garden
N Colonial Garden
O Magenta and Silver Garden
P Medieval Garden
Q Silver Garden

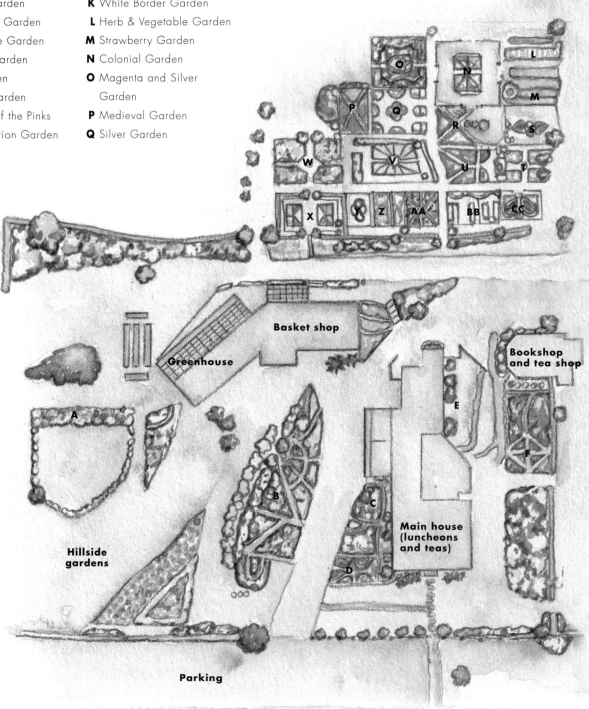

Basket shop

Greenhouse

Bookshop and tea shop

Main house (luncheons and teas)

Hillside gardens

Parking

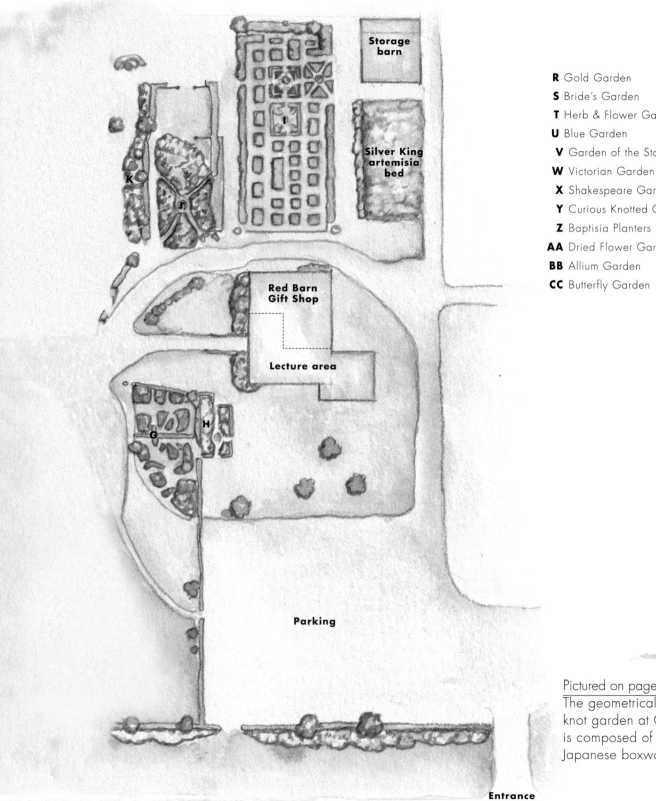

R Gold Garden
S Bride's Garden
T Herb & Flower Garden
U Blue Garden
V Garden of the Stars
W Victorian Garden
X Shakespeare Garden
Y Curious Knotted Garden
Z Baptisia Planters
AA Dried Flower Garden
BB Allium Garden
CC Butterfly Garden

Storage barn

Silver King artemisia bed

Red Barn Gift Shop

Lecture area

Parking

Pictured on pages 180–181: The geometrically patterned knot garden at Caprilands is composed of rue and Japanese boxwood.

Entrance

Not only did Adelma become an expert herb gardener and a wonderful herbalist, but she was also a font of information about the lore and history of herbs and herb gardening. She could readily cite cases and stories from merry old England, the Middle East, and the Far East. She was acquainted with traditional herbal usages all over the world. An herb walk with Adelma was more than an introduction to plants; it was also a history lesson. She became a much requested speaker at a variety of garden shows and herb conferences.

For Adelma, herbs were not just for show. As much as she appreciated their beauty, the more tangible attributes appealed to her as well. The flavors that herbs could add to a meal and the fragrances and colors that they brought to a home were of particular importance to her. She eventually created three gift shops on the grounds. One offers dried flowers harvested from the gardens, in bunches, arrangements, and wreaths. In the main barn you can find other harvests from the garden, in the form of teas, seasonings, and potpourri, as well as items from around the world, such as linens and pottery, featuring herb themes. What used to be the chicken coop became the cozy bookstore. Adelma's many musings in books and booklets are sold there, as are a grand selection from other herb authors.

The luncheons at Caprilands are legendary. Reservations must be made months in advance to secure a seat. The meals are served on the bottom floor of Adelma and Edward's house. The dishes are fantastically festive affairs, filled with fresh flowers, herbs, and vegetables culled from the gardens. If you have never experienced one of Caprilands' incredible meals, we can assure you that you will be hard-pressed to find a more colorful — and delicious — dining experience.

▷ Luncheon at Caprilands is served in several rooms downstairs in Adelma and Edward's home. Our favorite room, shown here, is decorated in olive green and pinks. Pomanders gaily strung with ribbons hang from the ceiling, and fresh flowers adorn every table. It is a warm, welcoming, festive atmosphere in which to dine.

Adelma divided the year into five seasons, rather than the typical four, citing Christmas as a season all its own, with its own sensibility, colors, sights, fragrances, and experiences. She considered Christmas to be the peak of the gardener's year, a busy, festive time when the ingenious herb gardener can call on his or her garden to provide many of the things that help create a joyous atmosphere. During the holiday season her home and garden were filled with sweet-scented evergreen and dried-flower wreaths, brilliant fabrics, glimmering candles, and a host of specially prepared seasonings for the glamorous feasts.

It seems fitting that Adelma passed on during the Christmas season. She was a true Christmas spirit, and her love for this particular season shines through in her writings.

When Shatoiya went to Caprilands the first time, she was so moved by its ambience and beauty that she cried. She felt a kinship with Adelma as a woman with a desire to work with nature to create something beautiful and then share the bounty. At that time, Dry Creek Herb Farm was just three years old, and Shatoiya anguished at the disparity between the two gardens. Her traveling companion reminded her of the great difference in the ages of the gardens, which lifted the dark cloud. She no longer felt dismayed by the relative smallness and newness of her garden, but instead was filled with renewed hope and vision for her efforts.

So, budding gardeners, take note: Even Caprilands, perhaps the most famous of all herb gardens, took almost fifty years to come to fullness. Like Adelma, and like herb gardeners everywhere, concentrate on building one step at a time; with perseverance, your grand vision will come to life. Remember that you are creating a legacy. The trees or herbs you plant today may become the enjoyment of generations beyond your lifetime.

◁ A purple martin house is surrounded by shrub and climbing roses.

◁ The shade of a hickory tree offers an intimate setting for viewing the gardens or having tea.

Pan in the Silver Garden

Many people's impressions of what an herb farmer should be are based, at least in part, on Adelma Grenier Simmons. She is without argument the Queen Mother of North American herbalism. Her flair and zest for life set the standard to which other herb gardeners aspire. Those fortunate to have known her were blessed by her vision. When Adelma passed on in December 1997, the herb world lost one of its most significant participants.

Adelma's husband, Professor Edward W. Cook, continues to carry on Adelma's work at Caprilands. His devotion to her memory is an inspiration to all who visit. Anyone who has ever walked these lovely gardens and had his or her soul replenished, if even just a little bit, owes a debt of gratitude to Adelma. Those who have never seen Caprilands but have benefited from some herbal remedy also owe Adelma a passing thought of thanks, for without her vision, perseverance, and eloquence the herbal renaissance would not be what it is today. Adelma paved the way for many of today's herbalists.

Who was Adelma Grenier

Simmons? As a child, Adelma was precocious and mischievous. Her father was a barber, and she was known from time to time to hide under the steps of his barbershop; from this hiding spot she would ambush unsuspecting customers with a soaking from the garden hose.

When she was a child, her parents thought some religious schooling might do some good, and they sent her off to church to get the "fear of God" put into her. Adelma brought her bulldog Buster with her. His habit of biting the ankles of the other parishioners got her quickly sent home and politely invited not to return with Buster, ever again.

Adelma was proud of the years she spent as a young woman working in the world of department-store purchasing. Her presence raised many an eyebrow: At the time, she was one of only two women in the male-dominated field. However, raising eyebrows seems to have been a lifelong avocation for Adelma. She had an eccentric and free nature. When she first moved to Coventry, she startled the community by painting her old house black, then covering that with a coat of red, creating an effect that was wild and witchy. At that time, Coventry was a collection of traditional, beautiful white New England homes. Although striking, the new paint job did not fit in with the local style.

Establishing a garden dedicated solely to herbs again raised eyebrows, as did Adelma's marriage to a very handsome but much younger man. But Edward Cook, well educated and respected, was a perfect complement to Adelma. A lesser man would never have held up to the bright light that was Adelma Grenier Simmons.

▷ The fine food served at Caprilands has its origins in the gardens. Here vinegar is infused with herbs in preparation for making salad dressing.

Adelma was a woman of many passions, and one of these was fine food. Anyone who has experienced a meal at Caprilands will attest to her love of great cuisine. She appreciated a good steak and claimed to have no use for chicken or fish. Vegetarians who assumed that her love for green things meant she must also be a vegetarian were quickly set straight; if they came to her wanting to discuss the benefits of vegetarianism, Adelma would put her chin on her chest and feign falling asleep until the transgressor wandered away. Then she would "reawaken" and continue whatever she had been doing.

Herbalist and author Jim Long was fortunate to cross paths with Adelma many times. He likes to recall one dinner in particular that illustrates her renowned marketing skill. During the course of the meal Adelma regaled the table with charming anecdotes about five different dishes served at Caprilands. The following day Jim went down to the gift shop eager to find the recipes for the dishes Adelma had talked about the night before. To his dismay, he found that each recipe was in a different cookbook. He had to buy five different books to get all the recipes Adelma had mentioned!

In her signature cap and cape,
Adelma cut a striking figure. Though she rarely acquiesced to photographs, she loved to be in the spotlight; she was a charismatic speaker and an extraordinary ambassador for herbs. Those closest to her knew Adelma to be an independent spirit, unaffected by the whims of culture or the pressure to conform. Her vibrant and passionate public persona was an accurate extension of her true soul.

△ Adelma and friends enjoy a quiet moment in a warm patch of autumn sunshine.

◁ A beautiful ash tree just beyond the nursery is one of the grandest attractions at Caprilands. It is at this spot that Adelma Simmons asked that her ashes be spread. She wished to become a part of the earth and, in so doing, a part of everything. When visiting there, we envision Adelma's spirit presiding over Caprilands through the far-reaching limbs of the giant ash tree, knowing that she will continue to inspire herbalists for years to come.

Adelma's Favorite Herbs

Adelma loved many, many herbs, but Professor Edward Cook tells us that she felt especially passionate about artemisia, thyme, and rosemary. We've profiled rosemary on page 58. Artemisia and thyme follow here.

Artemisia

We were overjoyed to learn that Adelma's favorite garden is also our favorite — the Silver Garden. In this garden, a circle of white stones is surrounded by plantings of silver artemisias and salvias. The white stones enhance the glimmer of various shades of silver. Set in the center of the circle is a delightful statue of a young Pan playing his pipes.

Adelma favored Silver King (*A. ludoviciana* 'Silver King') and Silver Queen (*A. ludoviciana* 'Silver Queen') artemisias for wreath making. She grew them in a "working" garden; the artemisia harvested from this garden served as a base for the wreaths sold in her gift shops.

Traditional Uses

Silver King and Silver Queen artemisias are both beautiful and aromatic. They retain their shape, color, and gentle scent when dried, which makes them a perennial favorite for potpourris and herbal wreaths. *A. ludoviciana* is not traditionally used for medicinal purposes, although it has many cousins that are, including mugwort *(A. vulgaris)*, wormwood *(A. absinthium)*, qing hao *(A. annua)*, southernwood *(A. abrotanum)*, and tarragon *(A. dracunculus* var. *sativa)*.

In the Garden

Silver King and Silver Queen artemisias are beautiful and hardy perennials that grow in tall spikes reaching up to 2 feet. Their lanceolate foliage is a striking silvery gray, ghostly color. In summer, the tips of the herbs' spikes bloom in that same hue.

Artemisia is a vigorous grower and tolerates a variety of soil conditions. It especially thrives in moist, fertile soil with lots of sun. But perhaps thriving isn't exactly what you want — Silver King and Silver Queen artemisia may overrun their neighbors if they are not contained. To contain artemisia, either install a barrier wall around its allotted space to keep roots from spreading or ruthlessly cut back spring shoots. You should also divide established plants every other year.

You can start artemisia from seed — purchase a packet from a reputable seed supplier and follow the package directions. However, taking a cutting from a living plant will produce results more quickly. Check in with commercial herb gardens in your area to see if they have cuttings available.

Harvesting

Harvest stalks as they bloom to maximize scent and capitalize on the pretty floral spike and its unusual texture. Spikes can be bundled and hung, covered with a paper bag to retain the scent and keep off the dust, until the stalks are completely dried.

Caprilands herbal wreaths

ARTEMISIA *ARTEMISIA LUDOVICIANA*

Plant Cycle: Perennial, Zones 4–8

Propagation: Artemisia is easy to propagate from cuttings, or it can be started from seed.

Parts Used: Aerial parts

Thyme

Thyme was another of Adelma's favorite herbs. Thyme has so many species and uses that it could provide enough material for a book all by itself. There are hundreds of species of thyme, and the correct naming of them is a heated subject among botanists.

Traditional Medicinal Uses

Garden thyme *(Thymus vulgaris)* is the species most often used medicinally. Its leaf is an effective antimicrobial that has a special affinity for the respiratory system. Thyme steams help loosen and expectorate phlegm, and thyme is often an ingredient for teas to heal the respiratory system. Thyme teas added to the bath are helpful in both treating and preventing colds. When a cold is making the rounds, we take a thyme bath once or twice a day.

Aside from baths, the best home medicinal use of thyme is to add the leaves, fresh or dried, as seasoning to your foods. During cold season, this will offer some immune protection. Like all "spaghetti" herbs, thyme is an antioxidant, helping to prevent a whole host of diseases, including cancer. Thyme is also a carminative, helping us to digest our food properly.

The essential oil of thyme has a high concentration of powerful chemicals and is potentially toxic. It should be used only externally, with caution, and always diluted. Thyme essential oil is antiseptic, antifungal, and antioxidant and is a specific vermifuge.

In the Garden

Thyme is an herb we often recommend to beginning herb gardeners. It thrives on neglect, is not too picky about soil, and will give you a reasonable harvest the first year. Being a Mediterranean native, thyme prefers full sun and a light, well-drained soil. However, we have had tremendous luck with it even in our hard clay soil.

In her writings, Adelma noted that she trimmed her thyme to about 3 inches high before the winter and mulched it heavily to protect it. In areas where the winter is very cold, frost can burn the leaves and frost heaves can damage the centers of the plants. Thyme roots can go as deep as 2 feet, though, so new leaves may come back strong in the spring as the energy rises.

After three or four years, thyme tends to die in the center and grow away from the middle in clumps, making this a good time to divide the plants.

THYME SCONES

Great with salads and cheese, these can be eaten hot or cold.

    8 ounces whole wheat flour
    ½ teaspoon baking soda
    ½ teaspoon salt
    1½ ounces butter
    3 tablespoons chopped fresh thyme
    ½ cup yogurt

Preheat the oven to 400°F. Mix together the flour, soda, and salt. Cut in the butter, then add the thyme. Make a well in the center of the mix and spoon in the yogurt. Mix and knead lightly. Press the dough into a 7-inch floured round pan. Score the top into 12 triangles. Bake for 30 minutes, or until scones are golden brown.

THYME *THYMUS* SPP.
Plant Cycle: Perennial, Zones 5–9
Propagation: Thyme is slow to
  start from seed, so we recommend
  taking cuttings or divisions.
Parts Used: Aerial parts

Saso Herb Gardens

a green oasis in silicon valley

Louis and Virginia Saso started their herb garden over thirty years ago on a rural road outside San Jose, California. Now their Saso Herb Gardens is a green oasis in the growing high-tech region known as Silicon Valley. The Sasos' welcoming nature and desire to share their knowledge of herbs earned them the love and respect of their community. They are often sought out as featured speakers for herb conferences, and their gardens are full of plants given to them by admirers from all over the world. By their example in living a healthy and natural lifestyle and through their apprenticeship programs and classes, Louis and Virginia have inspired several generations of herb gardeners and herbalists.

◁ Saso Herb Gardens is an intensely gardened one-acre plot insulated from the surrounding metropolis by a cushion of dense herbs. Standing within the confines of the garden, it is hard to imagine that you are in the middle of a bustling industrial region.

Just as Adelma Simmons's Caprilands gardens sparked a generation of herbalists in the northeast corner of the United States, so Saso Herb Gardens inspired those on the West Coast. Louis and Virginia Saso's gardens are an encouraging example of what can happen when you follow your heart and take steps to live a healthy and joyful life. That Louie and Virginia are doing what they truly love can be felt in every inch of their gardens.

Louie and Virginia are a joy to meet. As we first strolled the grounds with them, they introduced each plant as if it were an old friend, often having a special story to tell about how that plant came to their lives. They showed us with pride the *Salvia elegans* v. 'Louis Saso', which was cultivated by a former student to honor Louie.

Louie becomes noticeably more and more excited as he speaks of recent and future garden projects, his enthusiasm bringing a definite sparkle to his eye. His excitement in the garden is contagious enough to send anyone home eager to develop a relationship with his or her own backyard.

But Louie and Virginia weren't always herb gardeners. In fact, they didn't even start their herb gardens until Louie was in his late fifties. Before they came upon this avocation, which they both say has given them the best years of their lives, Louie owned a wholesale produce business in Hayward, California.

The produce business at that time was very competitive and cutthroat. Louie had to get up at 3:00 A.M. every day to work in a dog-eat-dog world. The hours and the stress were taking a toll on him, and he felt he was compromising his health. In the thick of raising eight children, Louie wanted to be sure that he would be around for them and his future grandchildren. He desperately needed a lifestyle change.

This was in the early 1970s, when there was renewed interest in gardening of all kinds, especially herb gardening. Inspired by Taylor's Herb Gardens near San Diego, Marquard Gardens in Santa Rosa, and Caprilands in the East, Louie and Virginia decided to try their hand at herb gardening. They found that they could make a bit of money selling small potted herb plants at local food cooperatives and farmer's markets. As their garden grew and prospered, Louie and Virginia gradually shifted their emphasis toward making a living from gardening.

▷ A beautifully carved, life-size statue of Saint Fiacre, the patron saint of gardeners, serves as the centerpiece of Louie and Virginia's gardens. As a seventeenth-century monk and herbalist, Saint Fiacre became renowned for his healing work with both the poor and the well-to-do. As his reputation grew, the bounty of his small garden became insufficient to supply his need for healing herbs. He went to the bishop to beg for more land. The bishop told him that he could have all the land that he could till in one day. Fiacre miraculously turned a tremendous amount of soil in a day, uprooting and clearing enough brambles and trees to make room for both a garden and a monastery.

One of the first challenges the Sasos faced was the soil: hard clay throughout the property. Louie was acquainted with the work of Alan Chadwick, one of the founders of the biointensive gardening movement. On the basis of Chadwick's recommendations, Louie planted tomatoes and sunflowers to break up the hard clay soil, making it easier to compost and to prepare it for other crops.

When the tomatoes and sunflowers had done their job, he took off the top layer of soil and planted more tomatoes. He did this several times, saving the topsoil each time. When he had all the topsoil he wanted, he amended it with the compost he had been making and put it back in the garden beds.

Louie made the acquaintance of a local rabbit farmer and offered to take the rabbit droppings off his hands. This he used to make organic compost — lots and lots of compost.

The gardens grew by trial and error, each experience offering Louie and Virginia a quality, hands-on education. At one point a friend suggested that Louie share his knowledge by offering a class on herb gardening through the local community college Extension program. The first workshop was held at West Valley Junior College in 1975, and thus Louie's herb teaching career began.

After the success of that first workshop, entitled "The Fascinating World of Herbs," Louie began offering classes at Saso Herb Gardens. An ancient oak tree

Saw palmetto

BIOINTENSIVE GARDENING

Alan Chadwick was one of the pioneers of biointensive gardening in North America. He believed that intensive gardening could improve the output of a parcel of land by a factor of four or more. A number of research centers around the continent are proving him right. Originally developed in France during the 1800s, biointensive gardening involves using smaller garden plots and managing them much more intensively than is called for in current gardening techniques.

Make your garden plot small enough that you can reach the entire garden from the sides without actually setting foot on the precious soil. Grow your plants right next to each other so they can support their green neigh-bors as they grow. There are many books on companion planting, so you can easily learn what plants should grow next to each other — and what plants shouldn't!

Turn and amend the soil to a depth of at least 2 feet, which allows the roots of the plants to run deep rather than spreading out. This, in turn, allows for closer spacing of the plants. The leaves of neighboring plants touch and form a microclimate on the garden floor that is conducive to plant production and is a deterrent to weed growth.

For more information, we suggest reading *How to Grow More Vegetables Than You Ever Thought Possible on Less Land Than You Can Imagine*, by John Jeavons.

serving as a gigantic umbrella for a brick patio creates Louie's outdoor classroom. With several picnic tables and some benches to sit on, it is the ideal place to learn about caring for the herbs.

At the same time that Louie began gardening classes, interest in wreath making, potpourri, and growing and using everlasting flowers was booming. Virginia has great talent in these crafts, so she started offering classes and workshops of her own. Virginia teaches her classes in a small barn adjacent to the nursery, the walls covered with her latest creations.

Over the years, interest in the medicinal use of herbs grew, and as it did the Sasos brought in established herbalists to teach classes and workshops on these uses. These forums launched the careers of many of North America's best-known herbalists, such as Christopher Hobbs and Michael Tierra.

As their business grew and became more successful, Louie and Virginia found that the workload was becoming too much even for them. So in 1984 they began an apprenticeship program. Participants in this eight-week program work in the morning, and in the afternoon they are offered instruction in such subjects as plant identification, compost making, and propagation.

There is no fee for this program. Students, like the apprentices of the old guilds, work for what they learn. It is a time-honored, hands-on tradition of the transfer of knowledge. Many of these apprentices continue working for the Sasos on a volunteer basis. It is the work of these generous individuals that helps Virginia and Louie maintain the beauty and quality of their gardens.

△ Virginia makes beautiful wreaths from the ornamental oreganos, artemisia, yarrow, and other flowers of her garden. Her expertise is well known, and she teaches regular classes for both novice and experienced crafters.

Near the front entrance to the property is the first herb garden the Sasos planted, an astrological garden. Using Culpeper's astrological gardening guide (see the box on page 28), Louie and Virginia planted twelve gardens like twelve slices of pie, each radiating from a central circle. The center of this garden is graced with a 5-foot wooden statue of Saint Fiacre, the patron saint of herb gardens. This rendition of the saint has become a mascot for the gardens. One of Louie and Virginia's daughters has created small plaster-cast statues of the saint to sell in the nursery, and they can be found in gardens all over the world.

The beauty of Saso Herb Gardens is the product of lots of hard work. But beauty has its price. Making a living with herbs is rewarding but also difficult. As Louie hints, if you undertake herb gardening as a career, don't "quit your day job" until your gardens are established and bringing in income.

According to the Sasos, creating a good herb garden requires a healthy partnership. There is just too much work for one person to build and maintain a quality herb and vegetable garden larger than a single 4-foot by 8-foot bed. If you're thinking of turning your entire backyard into an herbal paradise, make sure that your partner shares your vision and love for plants. Otherwise, you may find yourself scaling back your plans.

Ornamental oregano

Pictured on pages 202–203: The "zodiac" beds are labeled with small painted wooden signs and filled with brightly colorful herbs.

◁ The Sasos' astrological garden features a display bed for each sign of the Zodiac. Their design has been emulated at EverGreen Herb Garden (see page 115), among others.

Louie and Virginia's decision to change their profession was simply a small step in a larger process of bettering their lifestyle. The pressure and stress of their previous life had led them into a number of unhealthy lifestyle choices. When they took up herbs as a profession, they also decided to make other changes to benefit their health and lives. They both gave up cigarette smoking and coffee. They became vegetarians, and Virginia's flair in the kitchen proved that vegetarian fare can be hearty, robust, and flavorful.

At that time, vegetarianism was something that young people seeking an alternative lifestyle were following — most middle-aged folks had little or no interest in it. But Louie and Virginia saw it as a way to improve their health; it was not something they did because it was "trendy." In fact, the only time Virginia and Louie are "trendy" is when the rest of the population catches up to them. Then for a short time they are "with it," until everyone else goes on to the next fad, leaving Virginia and Louie being themselves as they always were and always will be.

There is an old saying that "you are what you eat." The Sasos are firm believers in eating the highest-quality foods available. Louie and Virginia stress growing your own food, especially if you are a vegetarian, because the quality of the soil and the growing conditions of the plants directly affect the nutritional value of the harvest from your garden. They feel that

eating the quality fruits and vegetables from their gardens has had a dramatic effect on their health and enjoyment of life.

Growing organically is vital for the Sasos. This is why Louie has spent so much time working to improve the quality of his gardens' soil. In addition to cultivating an abundance of herbs and vegetables, the Sasos grow several types of berries and have a variety of fruit trees. Louie enjoys grafting and has one apple tree bearing eight types of apples!

△ The Gemini "spoke" of the astrological garden features bright and beautiful geraniums.

◁ A small version of Saint Fiacre presides over a wheelbarrow planter overflowing with lively flowers.

The Sasos embody many of the attributes we often ascribe to Norman Rockwell's America. They are honest, hardworking, and generous. They hold a strong belief in serving the community, in giving back something of themselves to those less fortunate and to those who supported them when they needed it.

Not only are Louie and Virginia wonderful as individuals, but they also make an absolutely delightful couple. After all, you don't raise eight kids without learn-ing a thing or two about your partner. If you can survive that challenge, you can accomplish almost anything together.

This is not to say that they are two peas in a pod. Louie and Virginia are very different people. Virginia is like the honeybee. She flies about the garden checking in on this plant or that flower, always in motion, always on the go. Louie moves at a slower pace. He takes in his surroundings and notices the little changes taking place all around his garden.

A good partnership is not about being twins; it's about knowing your partner's strengths and weaknesses. It's about leaning on your partner's strengths and helping him or her with weaknesses. Virginia and Louie accomplish this with flair. Each is a perfect complement to the other.

The Sasos have a great following of former students and customers who have developed a genuine fondness and admiration for them. These feelings are reciprocated by Louie and Virginia, who consider themselves fortunate to have met so many wonderful people since they started their herb business. They feel that people who have a connection with plants and gardening share a special connection with each other.

The house that Louie and Virginia bought was originally a country home. The city now surrounds them, but Louie and Virginia remain undaunted, holding true to the vision that sent them to the country looking for a better way of life. Their one-acre garden and home have become an oasis in the booming Silicon Valley. They have turned down several offers to sell the property for considerable sums of money.

Going to Saso Herb Gardens is akin to a trip to Grandma and Grandpa's house — the home has the feeling of an old farmhouse. Eight kids were raised in this home; it has had a lot of living in it, and all that living has left its impression — small dents in the floorboards where an errant tricycle might have ventured, little marks that are evidence of the lives that grew up in this home. You can almost hear the shouts of joy and laughter that follow children wherever they live. Look at the stairway and see a young woman making an entrance in a new prom dress while her youthful suitor admires the descent from below. Life permeates this place; it is the difference between a house and a home. The Sasos have created a home; it is warm, welcoming, and comforting.

As they grow older, the Sasos are opening the gardens to the public less and less. They have taken great enjoyment in being able to share the work they've done in their garden, but now want more time for each other and their family. But they never see a time when they won't be working in their garden. In fact, they both have many ideas that they still wish to realize in their little Eden. They speak of incorporating more color into their garden, and Louie wants to continue experimenting with his fruit trees. Whether or not Saso Herb Gardens stays open to the public, it will remain an important reservoir of the "green energy" so desperately needed to balance the concrete world going up around it. And Louis and Virginia Saso, our mentors and good friends, will remain beloved and remembered by generation upon generation of herb growers.

Oregano blossoms

◁ An exuberant spray of lavender adds to the palette of vivacious colors at Saso Herb Gardens. Louie and Virginia, like most gardeners, love lavender for its beauty, its fragrance, and its multitude of uses.

The Sasos' Favorite Herbs

When we asked Louis and Virginia to name their favorite herbs, they of course chose oregano — the tumultous display of oregano blossoms on the edge of their garden could have told us that. They also picked out lemon verbena, which we profile here, and lavender, which is on page 116.

Lemon Verbena

Tolkien fans, take heart! This gracious plant may be a living remnant of Middle Earth. Lemon verbena is said to be the favorite herb of the Fairy Queen, who left this fragrant, treelike bush for our world as a remembrance of times past.

We were quite pleased to learn that lemon verbena is one of Louie and Virginia Saso's favorite herbs. Two sixteen-year-old bushes grace the fragrance garden at Dry Creek Herb Farm and are the highlight of our summer garden tours. Everyone takes home a leaf in his or her pocket, and the scent of this single leaf will last for days.

LEMON VERBENA CAKE

A white or yellow cake mix recipe
2 cups finely chopped lemon verbena leaves

Heat to a simmer the liquid portion (usually water or milk) of the cake recipe. Remove from heat, stir in the lemon verbena leaves, cover, and steep 10 minutes. Then uncover, let cool, and mix together the cake ingredients according to the recipe instructions, adding both the infused liquid and leaves as called for. Bake as directed, and enjoy.

Traditional Medicinal Uses

There are some historical references to lemon verbena's use as a digestive aid. We use lemon verbena mainly as a flavorful additive to our medicinal teas to make them taste, well, less medicinal. Lemon verbena can cover up the most awful flavors. Its sweet lemon scent and flavor are favorites of many herbalists.

Growing and Using

Lemon verbena is a tropical herb at heart; it is a garden plant in only the warmest regions, and must be brought indoors before any hint of frost.

Lemon verbena enjoys full sun and rich, sandy soil with good drainage. We give the plants a good mulching and cover them with a cold frame in late fall to protect their roots in winter. The leaves drop off in the winter, and the plants look absolutely dead. We have had students throw away live but dormant plants, thinking they had killed them!

In cooler climates, lemon verbena is the ideal plant for container gardens. It thrives in pots and looks quite at home growing on steps or along flagstone walkways. The plants can be taken indoors for the winter, though the leaves will still drop off and the plant will go dormant. Just water sparingly during the winter to keep the roots from completely drying up.

Lemon verbena's sweet scent was a favorite fragrance of Victorian ladies, and the toilet water made from its leaves graced many a dressing table. In potpourri, it brings indoors the romance of a summer garden. That lemon aroma also lends itself to tasty teas and confections.

LEMON VERBENA
ALOYSIA TRIPHYLLA
Plant Cycle: Shrub, Zones 8–11
Propagation: Lemon verbena can be started from cuttings.
Parts Used: Leaves and flowers

Oregano

Oregano is another of Louie and Virginia's favorite herbs. Oregano is cultivated worldwide, and there are many species, subspecies, and varieties. They are not easy to sort out. Also, what may be sold as dried culinary oregano in a market may not even be of the *Origanum* genus. It could be purposefully adulterated, or it just may be that one person's *Origanum* is another's *Lippia* or *Thymus*.

Sal Gilbertie, owner of Gilbertie's Herb Gardens in Westport, Connecticut, tells the story of an elderly Italian gentleman who came to Sal's nursery in search of an oregano plant. Sal proudly showed him a display of several varieties. The man plucked and smelled a leaf from each but shook his head: No, this was not oregano. Sal then took him to the marjorams, but these did not please the man either. Finally, Sal took him to the thymes. When the man pinched the leaves of oregano thyme (*Thymus* var.), he smiled and said, "Now *that's* oregano!"

Traditional Medicinal Uses

Ornamental oreganos are not usually used in cooking or medicine. However, *Origanum vulgare*, the common oregano used for both food and medicine, contains large amounts of thymol, which makes it a great herb to steam or bathe with to help prevent or heal respiratory problems.

O. vulgare and other "spaghetti" herbs (rosemary, thyme, garlic, basil) contain antioxidants, or free-radical scavengers. Free radicals occur when cellular atoms break down, losing electrons in the process. In an attempt to stay balanced, a free radical "borrows" an electron from a neighboring atom, setting up a cascading effect of electron thievery that can erode cell membranes and alter genetic material through oxidation. Free-radical formation can accelerate aging and has been linked to more than sixty diseases, including cancer. Antioxidants neutralize free radicals in the body, rendering them inactive. Supplements and foods rich in antioxidants, like oregano, support the body's ability to produce antioxidants and have a marked beneficial effect on human health.

Growing and Harvesting

Native to Eurasia and the Mediterranean area, oregano doesn't like wet feet and will do well in pots and raised beds. It prefers gravelly, well-draining soil. Although oregano is a sun-loving herb, potted plants may prefer some shade. Choose pots that allow the flower shoots to grow out and trail over the edge gracefully. You can also place the pots on pillars or place them on top of walls where the showy blossoms are free to cascade downward.

In the winter, trim back and mulch the plants. Potted plants should be placed near the house for some frost protection or, in colder climates, brought inside to sit in a sunny window.

Harvest the flowers for dried arrangements or wreaths while they are still tight buds or as they are just barely unfolding. Bundle in small bunches of six or seven stems and hang upside down to dry.

ORNAMENTAL OREGANO
*ORIGANUM LAEVIGATUM, O. ROTUN-
DIFOLIUM, O. 'KENT BEAUTY'*
Plant Cycle: Perennial, Zones 5–9
Propagation: Plants propagate
easily from cuttings or divisions.
Parts Used: Aerial parts

manifesting your own vision

It is always a pleasure to visit with herb gardeners and their gardens. Whether a simple backyard plot or an elaborate public display, these gardens are woven from common threads. These herbalists know their gardens as they might know their own children. Working with the intricacies of their gardens, they not only rely on classic gardening methods but also have discovered new gardening techniques that work for their particular microclimate. They understand their land and the needs of the plants that grow there. And by re-creating the spiritual and intimate connection these herbalists have with their gardens, you can, as they have, marry your own piece of land.

◁ The curving pathways and variety of textures offset the lush, manicured lawns of this garden, creating a green space that seems natural, a little bit wild, and definitely well loved.

Sitting with Your Land

A common thread of advice voiced by many of the gardeners highlighted in this book is to spend some time just experiencing your space or garden. Before you put a great investment of time and money into planning and building your herb garden, watch it go through all the seasons. Really get to know the rhythms of your piece of land.

Spending some time simply observing the land will save you a lot of mistakes. Watch for the details. During the wet season, is there a swampy part of your garden? There, consider growing plants that don't mind wet feet. Are there areas that seem dryer? You might design your irrigation system to account for them.

To really get to know your garden, use it as a meditation space. Just sit in the garden quietly, breathing slowly and listening to every little sound. This simple form of meditation calms the nerves and helps you get to know some of the energetic nuances of your garden space. But there are many forms of meditation. For some gardeners the simple act of putting a trowel in the ground or pulling weeds is a form of meditation.

Even if you take over the care of an established garden, get to know its pulse, its tempo. If you have the opportunity to speak with the prior caretakers, ask them the "whys" of the garden. Find out what they observed, and add that to what you see in the garden.

Foxglove

◁ Doing simple work in the garden is a form of service. It allows you to repay the land for the multitude of ways in which it serves you.

All life on this planet is, in some way or another, dependent upon the sun. Not only does the sun move from east to west each day, but as we change from season to season, the sun also moves higher or lower, depending on the time of year. All these cycles of the sun affect the sunlight available to your garden plants.

As a gardener it is crucial that you observe the movement of the sunlight's course across your land and situate your plants accordingly. Don't put a plant in the ground just because you think it will look nice in such-and-such a corner. If it doesn't get the sunlight it needs, or if it gets more sun than it can tolerate, it will not flourish, and it may die.

Budgeting Your Time

Every plant you put in your garden will need to be weeded, watered, fertilized, trimmed, harvested, put to bed in winter, and awakened in the spring. Just how many of these green beings do you want to be responsible for? If you haven't gardened before, start small, and see how much time you are able to give to the land. You will get as much harvest, if not more, from one properly cared for plant than from three that have had only slight attention.

We have watched over the years the garden of a distant neighbor we haven't even met. We drive by this garden weekly on our way to do errands in town. We have enjoyed observing his process. Each year he adds a section of garden or builds a new feature; the changes are subtle and slow. When he completes a garden, he works to include the maintenance of this new garden as part of the routine upkeep for the entire garden before he starts his next addition. Not until he is sure he can handle the additional work involved in supporting a new project does he start construction. In this way his garden grows in a natural manner, and he is sure that he will be able to take care of what he creates.

Don't rush headlong into your garden projects before making sure that you have the time and energy to care for them. Don't expect to create gardens comparable to Caprilands in one season. Know and understand that gardens like Caprilands have taken years and years to get where they are today. Most landscapers will tell you they plan four years ahead when they plot a new garden, and experienced gardeners will confirm that it takes four to five years for a garden to come into its own.

△ For healthy, abundant plants, take the time to observe the vagaries of sun and soil on your site, and plant accordingly. The lamb's ears outside our kitchen window thrives in the home we've found for it, which includes full sun and average soil.

Sharing with Friends

Sometimes it can be hard to see what's right in front of our nose. By inviting friends over to share your vision, especially those who are experienced in gardening in your area, you may receive some valuable advice and ideas. Have a garden party; make it a social event. Enlist the help of your guests in envisioning the future layout of your garden. Listen to their comments and be open-minded and flexible, but always keep an ear open to the voice of your heart and of your land.

Ritual Beginnings

Before you put that spade to the ground, you may want to do a ritual to consecrate your land. In some cultures, in fact, it is common for a couple to make love on the land before planting, to ensure fertility. An interesting concept — but potentially embarrassing to city dwellers with low fences.

Other time-honored traditions include saying a prayer and offering holy water, cornmeal, or tobacco. You could also sing, drum, or dance to stir up the heartbeat of your garden.

You could have a "garden warming," just like a housewarming. Friends could gather in a circle and each offer a prayer for your garden. Perhaps you would like a solitary ritual, including the quiet placing of a statue of a favorite saint.

Whatever you decide to do, all rituals come down to one important function: To take a moment to make the beginning of your garden special; to take a breath and honor your undertaking as a part of the healing of the earth and of yourself.

Taking a Look Around

Before you start planting, take stock of what grows wild in your neighborhood. Take a few walks around your property with a good field guide and see what wild plants you can identify. Even if you live in the city or suburbs, you should be able to find a vacant lot nearby; spend some time there learning what will grow in your neighborhood if given the chance.

Native plants are excellent indicators of many things that will affect your garden, such as how cold it gets in the winter, how hot it gets in the summer, how much frost you can expect, and the availability of water. You can learn these things and more by getting to know your native green neighbors.

Laying Out

Generally speaking, curves are more appealing than straight lines, and in gardens they're more productive. Gardens that are long and straight usually experience an energy loss at the ends of the rows, and plants there do not do as well. Round gardens maintain their energy throughout; however, it can be difficult to work the center of such a garden without treading on the precious soil near its edges. The shape of your garden may also be dependent in part on the materials you are building your bed with. If you're using wood, straight lines are simpler to make. More fluid, curving shapes are easier to create when using stone or just raised mounds of soil.

Resist the temptation to use railroad ties or pressure-treated wood to build raised beds. They are easy to use and long lasting, but railroad ties are often treated

△ Kokopeli, a Native American symbol, finds a fitting home among the brightly colored peonies.

with creosote and pressure-treated wood with chemicals. These toxins preserve wood but can leach into your soil and affect your plants. And actually, you don't even need to build up firm walls to contain your raised beds. You can simply mound the soil or follow the example of the Pilgrims at Plimoth Plantation (see page 92) and use branches, sticks, scrap wood, and whatever else is plentiful in your yard to contain the soil. Your plants will never know the difference.

Pictured on pages 220–221: An old wheelbarrow, the tried-and-true workhorse of the garden, stands among beautiful plantings of artichokes, peonies, daisies, and Spanish lavender.

▷ To add a sense of life and wildness to your container plantings, combine a variety of plants in one pot.

▷ Containers do not need to be confined to porches and patios. Set them out wherever a spot of color or greenery is needed, such as beneath a birdbath.

Container Gardening

When creating a container garden, there are several considerations to address. First, what kind of look do you want for your growing area? Are you setting the plants on an old-fashioned porch? Then perhaps you want white pots on pillars, with the herbs trailing down them. Or for a southwestern look, use terra-cotta strawberry pots or wooden boxes brightly painted with yellows, reds, greens, and turquoise. A fanciful container garden may use old washtubs, old farm equipment, barrels, and even old boots. (Of course, if you decide on these types of containers, make sure they haven't been treated inside with a substance that may harm your plants.)

Second, what materials are the pots made of? If you are using wood, redwood is the longest lasting in terms of resistance to rot. Terra-cotta pots "breathe" well, but they usually need more watering than other kinds of pots. Cheap clay pots that haven't been fired properly will crumble and chip easily.

In addition, think about where you'll be using the pots, and whether they need to be portable. When filled with dirt, wooden boxes and ceramic containers can be very heavy. Some large containers come with wheels attached or sit on trays with wheels for easy placement.

Very attractive plastic pots have come on the market recently. Plastic wears well and is light. However, some organic gardeners are concerned that when certain types of plastic sit in the heat, they can "outgas" chemicals that may go into the soil and your plants.

And you thought choosing the container was the easy part!

Now, which plants go in which pots? Generally, a plant needs an extra 2 inches of soil on all sides of its rootball. So you'll want to choose pots or containers that are appropriately sized for each plant. If you are going to put more than one plant in a container, be sure they have the same light and watering needs. Plant an herb that spreads voraciously (like mint), and that will end up taking over the whole pot, in its own container.

Even plants that like full sun when in the ground may need partial shade when grown in pots because there is no earth surrounding the plant to insulate the roots from the heat of the day. For this reason, some plants will also need water daily. Of course, much of this depends on the intensity of the sun and the humidity of your area.

A tiny teapot planter

Container gardening may sound like more work than it's worth. We feel, though, that one of the joys of container growing is that need to check in with your plants daily. This ritual can be your quiet down time, a chance to let the healing green energy soak in and surround you.

Remember, containers aren't for just the porch or patio. Properly placed, they make wonderful accents to your main garden. In fact, container gardening is the secret behind the lush look of many public gardens. Practiced gardeners often grow a multitude of plants in pots. They set some in holes in the ground in the garden and keep others in the greenhouse. Plants are rotated in and out of the garden as they need attention.

Whimsy in the Garden

A garden is not just a collection of plants. The most beautiful of gardens contain accents that highlight and enhance the appearance of the garden. We have been fortunate to have working for us a wonderfully inventive man named Andy. Andy has created a number of fanciful highlights in our gardens at little or no cost. When he finds an unusual rock, he sets it aside until he finds just the right place for it. We have a foot-tall Stonehenge he built from a number of angular rocks. He also created for us an upturned stump with its roots in the air supporting a collection of round rocks; we call it our stone tree.

Beautiful statuary is available at most nurseries and can add a lot to the appearance of most any garden. Our gardens feature a number of highly visible pieces that draw attention to themselves and the gardens where they sit, but what we really enjoy are the little touches that aren't noticed by anyone but the most observant visitors. These accents are like a private joke. Once you find one in the garden, you become more acutely aware of the details of the entire garden and search for more little secrets within.

Of course, sometimes a great idea for adding whimsy to the garden may not work out in a practical manner. Sal Gilbertie runs his family's fourth-generation nursery in Westport, Connecticut. It is a lovely nursery to visit, with display gardens all around the greenhouses and gift shop. Sal built model train tracks around his gardens and used to run his trains regularly to delight young visitors. Unfortunately, some of these guests liked pulling the trains off the tracks, and the Gilbertie R.R. runs no longer.

Benches and chairs add a wonderful touch to any garden. They invite the garden visitor to spend some time and enjoy the peace of the garden. Most gardeners put a great deal of consideration into the location of the bench but focus on where the bench will look best. What many fail to consider is the view from the bench. We've visited a number of benches in beautiful garden settings, only to sit down and have a wonderful view of the compost pile. Put your bench in a beautiful spot in the garden, but also put some time into creating a nice view from it.

The Garden Is Your Soul's Source

Gardening is much more than a simple exercise in providing food for the table, flowers for decoration, and medicines fo healing. Gardening is a way of recharging your soul. Gardening is a way to refresh your mind. To the deeply connected gardener, life without a garden is hardly worth living.

The gardeners featured in this book each have a slightly different approach to herb gardening, but they all have a true connection to their land. The reverence they hold for their gardens can almost be called spiritual. Their time spent in the garden is rejuvenating and life affirming.

Different styles of benches

A subtle garden ornament

Kwan Yin, the Chinese goddess of healing

Gazing ball

Wooden fowl

An elaborate sundial

resources

To Contact the Authors

**Dry Creek Herb Farm and
Learning Center**
Web site: www.drycreekherbfarm.com
*Shatoiya and Richard have moved their
herb gardens. To catch up with them, see
their schedule of classes and events, or
obtain a free mail-order catalog of bulk
herbs, books, and herb products, check
their web site.*

Public Gardens

Caprilands Herb Farm
534 Silver Street
Coventry, CT 06238
(860) 742-7244
*Gardens and gift shops open year round,
except New Year's Day, Easter Sunday,
Thanksgiving, and Christmas Day.
Hours are 10 A.M. to 5 P.M. from
December through March and 9 A.M. to
5 P.M. from April through November.
Lecture and five-course luncheon available as well as high teas; call for reservations. Mail-order catalog and calendar
of events available.*

**EverGreen Herb Garden and
School of Integrative Herbology**
P. O. Box 1445
Placerville, CA 95667
Phone/fax: (530) 626-9288
*Visits by appointment only. Call or write
for a free calendar of classes and events.*

Jim Duke's Green Farmacy
Although the Green Farmacy Garden is
not open to the public, private tours can
be arranged for a donation to the
garden fund of $2,000, or considerably
less for working weeding tours. All the
money generated from the tours is
plowed directly back into the garden, to
locate and purchase hard-to-find plants
and to help with the cost of maintenance. Those interested in volunteering
to work in the Green Farmacy Garden
should call (301) 428-8310.

Plimoth Plantation
P.O. Box 1620
Plymouth, MA 02362
(508) 746-1622
Fax: (508) 746-4978
Web site: www.plimoth.org
*Open daily 9 A.M. to 5 P.M., April
through Thanksgiving weekend. Mail-
order catalog of seeds available.*

Ravenhill Farm
1330 Mt. Newton X Road
Saanichton, BC V8M 1S1 Canada
(250) 652-4024
Fax: (250) 544-1185
*Open Sundays, 12 P.M. to 5 P.M., from
April through November.*

Sage Mountain
P.O. Box 420
East Barre, VT 05649
(802) 479-9825
Fax: (802) 476-3772
E-mail: sagemt@sagemountain.com
*Visits by appointment only. Call or write
for a calendar of classes and events.*

United Plant Savers Botanical Sanctuary
P.O. Box 98
East Barre, VT 05649
(802) 496-7053
E-mail: info@plantsaver.org

Mail-Order Seed and Plant Sources

Bountiful Gardens
19550 Walker Road
Willits, CA 95490

Companion Plants
7247 Coolville Ridge Road
Athens, OH 45701
(740) 592-4643

Dig This!
P.O. Box 5668 STN B
Victoria, BC V8R 5S4 Canada
(250) 370-0307
Fax: (250) 370-0337

Elixir Farm Botanicals
General Delivery
Brixey, MO 65618
(417) 261-2393

Gilbertie's Herb Gardens
7 Sylvan Lane
Westport, CT 06880
(203) 227-4175
*Open year-round from 8:30 A.M. to
3:30 P.M.*

Healing Spirits Herbs
9198 Rt. 415
Avoca, NY 14809
(607) 566-2701

Horizon Herbs
P.O. Box 69
Williams, OR 97544-0069
(541) 846-6704

Jean's Greens
119 Sulpher Springs Road
Newport, NY 13146
(315) 845-6500

Meadowbrook Herb Farm
Route 138
Wyoming, RI 02898
(401) 539-7603
Fax: (401) 539-7199
Store on site.

Nichols Garden Nursery
1190 North Pacific Highway
Albany, OR 97321
(503) 928-9280
Fax: (503) 928-8406

Peaceful Valley Farm Supply
P.O. Box 2209
Grass Valley, CA 95945
(888) 748-1722
Web site: www.groworganic.com
*Store and mail-order phone hours
9 a.m. to 5 p.m. PST.*

Richter's Herbs
357 Hwy 47
Goodwood, ON L0C 1A0 Canada
(905) 640-6677
Fax: (905) 640-6641
email: catalog@richters.com

Well Sweep Herb Farm
205 Mt. Bethel Road
Port Murray, NJ 07865
(908) 852-5390
Fax: (908) 852-1649

Books by Our Featured Gardeners

Cantin-Packard, Candis. *Pocket Guide to Ayurvedic Healing.* Freedom, CA: Crossing Press, 1996.

de la Tour, Shatoiya. *The Herbalist of Yarrow — A Fairy Tale of Plant Wisdom.* Sacramento, CA: Tzedakah Publications, 1994.

Duke, James, Ph.D. *Dr. Duke's Essential Herbs: 13 Vital Herbs You Need to Disease-Proof Your Body, Boost Your Energy, Lengthen Your Life.* Emmaus, PA: Rodale Press, 1999.

Duke, James, Ph.D. *The Green Pharmacy.* Emmaus, PA: Rodale Press, 1999.

Gladstar, Rosemary. *Herbal Healing for Women.* New York: Fireside Books, 1993.

Gladstar, Rosemary. *Rosemary Gladstar's Herbal Remedies for Children's Health.* Pownal, VT: Storey Books, 1999.

Gladstar, Rosemary. *Rosemary Gladstar's Herbal Remedies for Men's Health.* Pownal, VT: Storey Books, 1999.

Gladstar, Rosemary. *Rosemary Gladstar's Herbs for Longevity & Well-Being.* Pownal, VT: Storey Books, 1999.

Gladstar, Rosemary. *Rosemary Gladstar's Herbs for Natural Beauty.* Pownal, VT: Storey Books, 1999.

Gladstar, Rosemary. *Rosemary Gladstar's Herbs for Reducing Stress & Anxiety.* Pownal, VT: Storey Books, 1999.

Gladstar, Rosemary. *Rosemary Gladstar's Herbs for the Home Medicine Chest.* Pownal, VT: Storey Books, 1999.

Richardson, Nöel. *In a Country Garden: Life at Ravenhill Farm.* Vancouver, British Columbia: Whitecap Books, 1996.

Richardson, Nöel, and Jenny Cameron. *Herbal Celebrations Cookbook.* Portland, OR: Graphic Arts Center Publishing Co., 2000.

Richardson, Nöel. *Summer Delights: Cooking with Fresh Herbs.* Vancouver, British Columbia: Whitecap Books, 1996.

Simmons, Adelma Grenier. *The Caprilands Wreath Book.* Coventry, CT: Caprilands Publishing Co., 1987.

Simmons, Adelma Grenier. *Herb Gardening in Five Seasons.* New York: Plume, 1992.

Tierra, Michael. *The Herbal Tarot Deck,* illustrated by Candis Cantin-Packard. Stamford, CT: United States Games Systems, 1997.

Yeoman, Andrew. *A West Coast Kitchen Garden: Growing Culinary Herbs and Vegetables.* Vancouver, British Columbia: Whitecap Books, 1996.

index

Profiled herbs are listed with their Latin names. Page numbers in *italics* indicate photographs.

Other Storey Books You Will Enjoy

The Family Butterfly Book, by Rick Mikula. Author Rick Mikula, the "grandfather of butterfly farming," shares his vast knowledge, contagious enthusiasm, and deep respect for these fascinating creatures. Readers will learn how to attract, safely catch, handle, and support butterflies as well as how to create a butterfly habitat and the basics of butterfly farming. The book also features close-ups, including photographs and illustrations of eggs, caterpillars, chrysalises, and butterflies, of forty favorite North American species. Adults and children alike will enjoy this exciting, intriguing, and environmentally important book. Paperback. Full color. 176 pages. ISBN 1-58017-292-X.

Growing 101 Herbs That Heal: Gardening, Techniques, Recipes, and Remedies, by Tammi Hartung. Herb grower and herbalist Tammi Harting offers in-depth profiles for growing 101 medicinal plants using totally organic techniques. Hartung shares all the secrets of propagation, soil preparation, natural pest management, harvesting, and even garden design for both beauty and highest yield. Readers will learn to make inexpensive, potent home remedies and recipes for the whole family by following Hartung's easy, step-by-step instructions. Paperback. Full color. 256 pages. ISBN 1-58017-215-6.

The Herbal Home Remedy Book: Simple Recipes for Tinctures, Teas, Salves, Tonics, and Syrups, by Joyce A. Wardwell. Author Joyce Wardwell helps reader identify and use twenty-five easy-to-find herbs to make simple remedies in the form of teas, tinctures, salves, tonics, vinegars, syrups, and lozenges. She gives hundreds of suggestions for maintaining health and well-being simply, naturally, and inexpensively. Folklore — including Native American legends and stories — provides information on the origins of many herbal medicines. 176 pages. Paperback. ISBN 1-58017-016-1.

The Herbal Palate Cookbook, by Maggie Oster and Sal Gilbertie. Two of the best-known names in the herbal field teamed up to create this collection of outstanding recipes featuring fresh herbs as their central ingredient. This beautiful full-color book offers 150 simple yet elegant recipes for appetizers, salads, soups, main and side dishes, breads and muffins, desserts, and drinks. An herb identification section contains color photographs and instructions for growing herbs in containers. Paperback. 176 pages. ISBN 1-58017-025-0.

Rosemary Gladstar's Herbs for the Home Medicine Chest, by Rosemary Gladstar. One of six titles in Storey's Rosemary Gladstar Collection. Rosemary provides concise, easy-to-understand, and practical information for using herbs for health and well-being. Readers will find herb profiles, cautions, contraindications, and easy-to-make recipes that should be stocked in every home medicine chest. Paperback. 80 pages. ISBN 1-58017-156-7.

These books and other Storey Books are available at your bookstore, farm store, garden center, or directly from Storey Books, Schoolhouse Road, Pownal, Vermont 05261, or by calling 1-800-441-5700. Or visit our Web site at www.storeybooks.com.